3 AM Grief

A Light for the Quiet Hour

Delilah Klug

ISBN (Paperback): 979-8-9940524-0-2
ISBN (eBook): 979-8-9940524-1-9
Interior design by: Delilah Klug
Published by 331 Enterprises

For inquiries or updates:
Email: **delilah@331enterprises.com**

PRINTED IN THE UNITED STATES OF AMERICA

DEDICATION

To the woman who refused to give up on herself -
Thank you for carrying me here.

CONTENTS

"Theres something sacred about the hours
between night and morning-
When everything feels broken, but somehow
you still breathe through it."

Delilah Klug

ACKNOWLEDGMENTS

To my husband, Dustin –
Thank you for loving me in a way that still
lights every room I walk into.
Your life, your laughter, your legacy live in
Every word I write.
I carry you with me into every page.
I hope to make you proud of the life I'm
Rebuilding for our children and me.

To my children –
You are my why.
Everything I build, everything I create,
Everything I fight through…
It all leads back to you.
I am honored to be chosen as your mother.

To the reader –
Thank you for picking up this book in your quiet hour.
If these letters brought you even one breath of comfort,
one moment of ease,
Or one reminder that you are not alone at 3 AM –
Then this book has done exactly what it was meant to do.

Letter One: When the Night Feels Endless

Dear Sleepless One,

It's 3 AM again.
The house is still.
Only the smallest sounds exist—
a refrigerator hum, a clock somewhere in the dark,
the faint reminder that time hasn't stopped even if it feels like it should.

If you're awake, it isn't failure.
It's simply what happens when life has been heavier than sleep.
The night makes room for everything the day couldn't hold.
That's all this is—
room.

You don't have to move.
You don't have to find meaning.
You don't have to reach for peace.

You can just exist.
Blanket pulled close,
pillow shaped to your memory,
eyes open or closed—either way, you're allowed to rest.

The world outside is quiet because it's supposed to be.
You don't have to meet anyone's expectations here.
You don't even have to meet your own.

Sometimes thoughts arrive uninvited.
They replay things you wish had gone differently.
They ask questions that have no answers.
Let them drift through; they'll pass on their own.
You don't need to fight them—only let them exist beside you.

This hour isn't a punishment.
It's a pause.
A soft pocket of time where nothing is required.

If the bed feels too big, that's okay.
It remembers what it held, too.
It's not emptiness you're feeling—it's evidence of love.
What remains after someone leaves
is proof they were once real in your world.
That feeling is the shadow of something that mattered.

There's nothing to chase tonight.
Not peace.
Not meaning.
Not sleep.

You've done enough for one day.
Let the dark wrap around you the way quiet does—
steady, familiar, almost kind.

If tears come, let them.
They don't change the truth of your survival.
If no tears come, that's fine too.
You don't owe your grief any particular shape.

The night will end eventually.
The light will shift.
But right now, you don't have to look toward morning.
You can stay exactly where you are
and still be moving forward in ways no one can see.

You're not behind.
You're not broken.
You're human.
And even when the world feels distant,
you still belong to it.

Just rest.
Not perfectly.
Not completely.
Just enough.

With you in the sleepless dark,
Delilah

Letter Two: The Body That Carries You

Dear Sleepless One,

There's a quiet fatigue that never really leaves.
The kind that sits in the bones,
in the shoulders that hold more than their share,
in the chest that sometimes forgets how to feel light.

Your body remembers everything—
the shocks, the long nights, the holding-it-together.
Even now, when you want it to relax,
it stays half-ready, half-guarded,
as if the next loss could arrive at any second.

It isn't weakness.
It's memory.

You've asked your body to keep going
when your mind couldn't.
You've carried groceries and guilt in the same hands.
You've smiled through heartbreaks,
swallowed exhaustion,
and pretended that shaking hands were steady.

You did what you had to do.
And that matters more than anyone will ever see.

Tonight, if you feel every ache at once,
don't turn away from it.
It's just the body speaking in its own language—
the way it tells you, *I'm still here.*

You don't need to correct it.
You don't need to explain it.

The body has its own form of truth,
and truth often arrives as tiredness.

Sometimes you wonder
how something so heavy can still move.
How the same heart that's been cracked
can still keep rhythm.

It does.
Quietly.
Without asking for credit.
It keeps time even when you don't want to.

There's tenderness hidden under the tension.
A soft pulse that still believes in tomorrow,
even when the rest of you isn't sure.

Let that be enough tonight.
Not healing.
Not progress.
Just proof that you are still made of life.

You don't have to admire your strength.
You don't have to turn this into gratitude.
You only have to notice that after everything,
you're still here—
and that's the closest thing to peace
this hour requires.

Your body has carried you through more than it ever should have had
to.
It will carry you through this, too.
Not perfectly.
Not quickly.
Just steady, the way it always has.

With you in the quiet strength beneath the tired,
Delilah

Letter Three: When Thoughts Won't Settle

Dear Sleepless One,

The mind never really sleeps.
Even when the body is still,
it keeps turning,
spinning through the day that's already over,
rearranging moments that won't fit anywhere else.

Sometimes it whispers.
Sometimes it shouts.
Sometimes it plays the same sentence again and again
until you forget what silence sounds like.

You don't have to stop the noise.
You don't have to make sense of it.
It's only the mind trying to find a place to
put all the things it couldn't carry in daylight.

That's what this hour becomes—
a hallway of unfinished thoughts,
a place where everything you tried to hold back
comes looking for space.

It isn't wrong.
It isn't a sign that you're broken.
It's just what happens
when a person has lived through too much
and still has more to understand than words can reach.

The mind does what it knows:
it circles.
It replays.
It checks the locks on memories
to see if they're still there.

If your thoughts are loud tonight,
let them exist without argument.
They will quiet eventually—
not because you forced them to,
but because even noise gets tired.

You don't have to join the search.
You can simply stay here,
beneath the swirl,
letting the hours pass the way water does around a stone.

When the noise softens—
and it will—
you'll notice something steady beneath it.
Not calm exactly,
but presence.
The kind that doesn't demand anything from you.

That's where you are now.
Not trapped in thought,
just alive enough to still have them.

And that's enough for tonight.

With you in the quiet hours,
Delilah

Letter Four: When the Weight Won't Lift

Dear Sleepless One,

There are nights when everything feels heavier than it should.
The air, the blankets, the thoughts that won't stop pressing down.
Even breathing feels like work.

It's not because you've done something wrong.
It's because the world asked too much of you,
and you kept saying yes because you didn't know how to stop.

Now your body carries what people couldn't see—
the words you didn't say,
the tears you saved for later,
the small moments that hurt but never looked like they should.

The weight isn't constant.
Some days you forget it's there.
Other days it returns without warning,
settling across your shoulders like a familiar shirt you never meant to
keep.

There's no switch to turn it off.
There's only time.
And the quiet understanding that you can exist with the heaviness
without becoming it.

You've probably tried to reason with it before.
You've told yourself to think positive,
to move on,
to be grateful,
to look for the lesson.

But some things don't need lessons.
They just need space.

Not to be solved,
just witnessed.

If it feels like the weight will never leave,
remember—everything you've ever carried has shifted, eventually.
Maybe not disappeared,
but moved.
Changed shape.
Found somewhere else to rest.

This will too.
Not because you'll wake up one morning and it's gone,
but because you'll wake up one morning
and realize you've grown strong enough to carry it differently.

There's nothing you need to do tonight.
You don't have to find the silver lining.
You don't have to name the pain.

You only have to allow this small truth to exist:
you are tired,
and that's reason enough to stop for now.

Let the weight be what it is.
Let the night hold it for a while.
You've done enough.

The heaviness doesn't erase your worth.
It doesn't mean you're failing.
It only means you're human—
someone who has loved,
lost,
tried,
and is still here.

And being here, even under all this weight,
is its own kind of courage.

With you when the world feels heavy,
Delilah

Letter Five: Everyday Weight

Dear Sleepless One,

Some days it's the small things that undo you.
The way the mail still arrives in both your names.
A task you used to do together
that now takes twice as long,
not because it's difficult-
but because it feels different.

You used to move through these moments without thinking.
Now they ask for thought, for effort, for courage.
Even something as simple like locking the door at night
feels heavier than it once did.

It's strange how the world keeps going
as if nothing stopped.
How grocery stores play the same music.
How the seasons still change.
How people laugh in meetings.
It almost feels cruel-
the life continues when yours feels paused.

But maybe the cruelty isn't in the continuation.
Maybe its in the reminder
that what used to be easy
now asks for so much of you.

You might find yourself frustrated.
You might whisper, I used to do this without thinking.
You might look at a sink full of dishes
and feel the weight of the entire past.
You're not overreacting.
You're remembering.

The smallest routines are built from shared rhythms.
And when one rhythm disappears,
the body stumbles trying to keep its own time.

Theres no need to rush back to "normal."
Normal doesn't live here anymore.
What exists now is quieter kind of life-
Different, slower,
shaped by everything you've lost
and everything you still are.

The things that used to be easy
will not always feel this hard.
But even when they do,
you don't have to meet them with perfection.

You can leave the laundry for tomorrow.
You can eat the same meal again.
You can skip the small talk.
You can let ease return when its ready.

Every ordinary thing you manage to do
is a kind of resilience.
Its how you rebuild-
not through grand gestures,
but through the quiet act of facing the day in front of you.

So if all you did today
was get through it,
that's enough.
That's something.

It may not look like progress,
but it is.
Because you're still here,
learning to move again in a world
that doesn't yet know how to move with you.

And that's how life starts over-
not easily,
but gracefully.

With you through the hard moments,
Delilah

Letter Six: Life Kept Going, and So did You

Dear Sleepless One,

You walk through familiar places,
but they don't feel familiar anymore.
The sidewalks haven't changed.
The streetlights still flicker in the same spots.
The coffee still tastes the way it always did.
But somehow, everything looks slightly off,
like the world was rearranged
while you weren't looking.

You stand inside it,
and you can't tell if it's the world that's different
or if it's you.

People wave the same way.
Neighbors ask how you've been
without really waiting for an answer.
And you give them the practiced smile—
the one that keeps conversations short,
the one that protects your energy.

You don't mean to seem distant.
You just don't fit the shape
the world remembers you being.

That's what grief does.
It redraws your edges.
It changes your sense of time,
your understanding of what matters,
your definition of okay.

Sometimes you miss the person you were
before everything shifted.

16

You miss how easily you used to laugh.
How light felt natural instead of borrowed.
How you used to wake up
without first bracing for the day.

You didn't choose to change;
it happened quietly,
in the moments when you were just trying to survive.

Now, you notice it everywhere—
in your reflection,
in your reactions,
in the way your silence feels heavier
but also, truer.

It's hard when the world expects you
to be who you were.
It doesn't see the difference between functioning
and feeling.
It doesn't understand that even small talk
can take everything you have left.

You're allowed to protect your peace.
You're allowed to take longer
to re-enter the spaces that used to feel safe.

You're allowed to grow past
the version of yourself that existed before.

You haven't disappeared.
You've evolved.
You've become someone who sees differently,
who listens deeper,
who notices what most people miss.

That awareness will feel lonely for a while.
But one day,
you'll find moments where it feels like clarity instead—
where you realize you haven't lost everything,
you've just learned to see what remains.

Tonight, if the world feels too unchanged
while you feel entirely new,
let that be okay.
You don't have to keep up with it.
You don't have to pretend it all fits.

You're not behind.
You're just rebuilding—
invisible to everyone but yourself.

And the world will catch up to you eventually.

With you as you grow where you once only survived,
Delilah

Letter Seven: When You Start to Feel Again

Dear Sleepless One,

It catches you off guard the first time.
A moment that doesn't hurt.
A quiet that feels peaceful instead of empty.
A laugh that escapes without warning.

You almost stop yourself,
as if joy should still be off-limits,
as if feeling better means forgetting.
But that's not what's happening.
It's just your heart stretching,
testing its edges,
seeing if there's still room for warmth.

For so long, everything inside you felt muted—
like colors washed in black.
Now, every small shift feels loud, unfamiliar.
A song you used to love doesn't sting as much.
A sunrise catches your attention.
The world looks a little softer,
and you wonder if it's okay to notice, it is.

You don't have to apologize
for feeling something other than pain.
You don't have to explain it.
Healing doesn't erase what happened,
it simply gives you small pockets of air
so you can keep breathing.

Some days, the air still feels thin.
You might laugh in the morning
and cry by noon.

That doesn't mean you're going backward.
It means life and loss
have learned how to share the same space.

You're not betraying the person you lost
by living.
You're honoring them every time you do.

The ache and the joy were never meant to cancel each other out.
They were meant to coexist.

It takes courage to let yourself feel again.
To risk softness after so much pain.
To let comfort touch you without flinching.

You've earned that courage quietly,
in all the nights you didn't think you could go on
and somehow still did.

You don't need to name this as progress.
You don't have to call it hope.
You can just let it be what it is—
a small reminder that your heart
still knows how to recognize light.

Tonight, if you catch yourself feeling something new—
don't overthink it.
Let it stay a little while.
Let it whisper quietly in the background

like a song you once knew.

You don't have to hold on tight.
You don't have to protect it.
You just have to let it exist.

Because it's proof that even after everything,
your heart is still alive enough to feel.

And that's how the world begins to come back to you—
not all at once,
but piece by piece,
as you begin to come back to yourself.

With you as you gently embrace the person you have become,
Delilah

Letter Eight: Living Again

Dear Sleepless One,

There comes a point when you start moving through the day
without thinking about how hard it used to be.
It doesn't mean it's easy now—
just that it's possible.

You wake up and realize
you've gone longer than usual without the heaviness pressing down.
You've made the coffee,
folded the laundry,
answered a message
without needing to convince yourself first.

You didn't plan it.
You just did it.
And that quiet return to motion
is one of the bravest things you'll ever do.

For a long time, even the simplest tasks felt impossible.
The world looked too sharp, too big, too loud.
You lived hour by hour,
just getting through what was right in front of you.
And that was enough.
It still is.

But somewhere along the way,

without realizing it,
you began to live *with* your pain instead of *inside* it.
You began to carry it instead of being carried by it.

That's not healing you can measure.
It's not the kind that earns applause.

But it's the kind that lasts.

You might still notice the absences everywhere.
The empty chair,
the unanswered text thread,
the plans that never happened.
They don't disappear,
but they stop being the only thing you see.

You start to notice other things again—
how light hits the floor in the morning,
how your hands still know how to steady themselves,
how laughter from another room
no longer feels like something happening to someone else.

This is what returning looks like.
Not celebration.
Not arrival.
Just slow, steady participation in life again.

You may worry that by living this way,
you're moving on too fast.
You're not.
You're just moving *with*.
With memory.

With ache.

With the understanding that life has kept going
and somehow,
so have you.

There's no finish line to cross.
No final version of peace waiting at the end.
There's just this—
a day that unfolds without falling apart.
A night that ends without breaking you open.

That's progress.
Even if no one else sees it,
your body knows.
Your heart knows.
And one day,
you'll know too.

So tonight,
don't question the small ways you're rebuilding.
Don't shrink them down to make the loss fit again.

It's okay to belong to your life
even while you still miss the one you had before.

This is how you learn to live inside your days again—
not perfectly,
not painlessly,
but fully enough
to remember that you're still here.

And that's all this world asks of you tonight.

With you while the world learns the new you,
Delilah

Letter Nine: The Quiet Days

Dear Sleepless One,

There are days when you almost forget to think about it—
when the noise of living takes up just enough space
to drown out the ache.

And then suddenly,
without warning,
it hits again.

Not a full collapse,
just a lump in the throat,
a small pause that reminds you:
the quiet still knows your name.

It happens in the middle of nowhere—
in line at the store,
in the car when a song you didn't expect starts playing,
in the kitchen when the light hits a certain way.
You stop,
and for a moment,
you're back inside the memory you thought had softened.

No one around you would notice it.
It's an invisible kind of grief—
the kind that surfaces in seconds
and leaves you breathless before you can explain why.

You don't owe anyone an explanation.
These moments are part of living now.
They're proof that memory is still alive
in the small corners of your world.

It doesn't mean you're going backward.

It doesn't mean you're broken again.
It means love still echoes.
It means your heart still listens.

You've built a life that holds both noise and quiet,
and every once in a while,
the quiet just wants to be heard.

There's a tenderness in that interruption,
even when it hurts.
Because it reminds you
that what you loved didn't vanish—it changed.
It's still moving with you,
woven into the way you notice beauty,
or pause longer at sunsets,
or feel everything deeper than before.

The quiet isn't punishment.
It's memory returning to say, *"I still exist."*

So when it catches you again,
don't fight it.
Don't rush to fill the space.
Let it pass through.
Let it speak its small truth:
that loss may soften,
but it never stops meaning something.

And neither do you.

The quiet will always come and go.
But you're learning that it doesn't have to undo you anymore.
It can visit,
stay a little while,
and then leave when it's ready—
like a wave that knows you now,
but no longer knocks you off your feet.

That's not weakness.
That's growth.

It's the quiet kind of strength
that doesn't announce itself,
but you can feel it—
in the way you stand again after the ache,
in the way you keep breathing when the memory fades.

That's what living after loss looks like.
Not forgetting.
Just learning how to stay steady when the quiet returns.

With you as you rise quietly,
Delilah

Letter Ten: On Nights That Won't End

Dear Sleepless One,

Some nights stretch farther than they should.
The clock moves, but it doesn't feel like it.
Minutes widen until they look like hours,
and the room holds everything you were trying not to feel.

It isn't because you're doing anything wrong.
It isn't a test you're failing.
It's just a long night—
the kind the body remembers
and the mind fills with echoes.

You notice sounds you miss in daylight.
A pipe settling.
A branch against the siding.
The refrigerator starting and stopping
like a distant tide.
The house has its patterns;
you're learning yours again too – how to belong in the stillness
without rushing it away.

There's a point where tired tips into wired.
Where the eyes are heavy
but the thoughts are awake.
Where you aren't sure if you want silence
or something soft to break it.

This is the part that feels endless.
This is the part that convinces you
morning forgot its way to your street.

If the bed feels too big,
it's because it's holding more than you can name.
Not emptiness—evidence.
A shape that used to be here.
A warmth the mattress remembers even now.

If you turn toward the space beside you,
it's not weakness.
It's reflex.
The body reaches for what it knew,
then learns again how to be only itself.
That learning takes time
no clock can measure.

Long nights have a way of collecting questions.
What if.
Why then.
Why this.
They don't need answers right now.
They can wait on the nightstand with everything else.
Not discarded—just set down
where they don't have to be held.

You don't owe the dark explanations.
You don't owe yourself certainty.
You can let the unknown be the unknown
without pulling it closer.

There's a kind of strength
that only shows up after midnight.
Not the loud kind.
Not the kind people clap for.
The quiet endurance of staying true to this moment
when the hours refuse to pass.

The steady choice to keep lying here,
even when the mind tries to rehearse
every version of the past.

Remaining is its own kind of courage.
Breathing without demanding anything back from the air
is a form of work no one sees.

You might remember how nights used to be easy.
How sleep arrived without negotiation.
How the day ended on its own.
That memory can ache.
It can also tell you something true:
you once knew how to rest.
That knowing didn't disappear;
it's just buried under all this feeling.
It will find you again—
not because you chase it,
but because rest still knows your name.

If tears come, they're only proof of weight.
If they don't, that's a kind of proof too.
Either way, nothing essential about you is changing.
You are not less for needing a softer hour.
You are not more when you get through without breaking.
You are simply a person
living through a night that refuses to hurry.

Sometimes memory arrives like weather.
A sudden gust.
A brief downpour.
It leaves the room different when it goes.
You don't have to read the sky.
You don't have to prepare a speech for the clouds.

You can let the weather be weather,
and let the room return to itself
in its own time.

What helps isn't always doing;
often it's permission you give yourself.
Permission to leave the thoughts unfinished.
Permission to let the dishes wait.

Permission to be exactly as human
as this hour allows.

The world isn't asking anything of you right now.
There are no forms to fill
in the space between 3 and 4. A.M
No one needs your answer before dawn.

If you worry that the night will always feel this long,
remember the nights that didn't.
They're easy to forget because they ended quietly.
They're evidence, not promise—
but evidence is enough here.
It says: some hours pass gently.
It says: this one will pass too,
even if it takes longer than you hoped.

When morning finally thinks of you,
it will not apologize for being late.
It will just open the room by a shade
and let the ordinary return—
a kind of mercy that never announces itself.

Until then, length is only length.
A measurement, not a verdict.
You are not being judged by how quickly you fall asleep,
or how calmly you hold the dark.

You are allowed to be tired of this.
You are allowed to want it over.
You are allowed to remain exactly where you are
and call that enough.

Let the night be long if it needs to be long.
Let your body be heavy if it needs to be heavy.
Nothing is required of you here
but the simple truth that you're still here.

And that truth is steady,
even when the hours are not.

With you in the sleepless dark,
Delilah

Letter Eleven: After the Long Night

Dear Sleepless One,

You made it through another night.
You might not have slept much.
You might have watched the clock drift past every hour.
But you're still here - and that counts.

The world outside your window looks the same,
but somehow the light feels softer—
like it knows what you've survived.
Morning doesn't fix anything,
but it reminds you that even the longest night
has an end.

You don't have to rush to meet the day.
You can stay right where you are for a while.
Let the quiet morning wrap around you
the way a blanket does—
not to erase the ache,
but to hold it gently.

You're allowed to move slowly.
You're allowed to begin again
without having to call it progress.
You're allowed to exist
without a plan for what comes next.

People will tell you mornings are for motivation,
for gratitude, for fresh starts.
But sometimes, mornings are simply for survival-
for sitting with a cup that's gone cold
because you were lost in thought.
For standing at the window
and letting the light fall on your face

just long enough to remember that you're still here.

That's enough for today.

If your body feels heavy,
don't mistake it for failure.
It's the weight of everything you've carried
meeting the light that doesn't judge you for it.
Even your exhaustion is proof
that you kept going when you could have stopped.

You are not behind.
You are not weak.
You're simply in the middle—
the night that tried to break you
and the morning that hasn't asked anything of you yet.

So before the world begins demanding,
let this be your moment of peace.
No expectations.
No performance.
Just you, breathing,
while the day unfolds slowly enough
for you to decide what it means.

You've already done the hardest part.
You stayed.

With you in the storm of thoughts,
Delilah

Letter Twelve: Safety in Small Things

Dear Sleepless One,

There's a certain kind of peace
that doesn't announce itself.
It doesn't come with confetti or revelation.
It arrives quietly,
disguised as something ordinary—
the faint noise of the refrigerator,
the warmth of your mug against your hands,
the soft stretch of daylight across the floor.

It's easy to miss,
especially after so much chaos.
You've spent so long waiting for the next wave to crash
that calm can feel suspicious—
like the silence before another storm.

But this quiet isn't a warning.
It's an offering.

You don't have to do anything with it.
You don't have to name it,
or question how long it will last.
You can simply notice it.
A small moment where your body
doesn't feel like it's fighting something.

That's all peace really is—
not perfection,
not permanent stillness,
just seconds where survival isn't the only thing you know.

You've learned how to exist in chaos.
You've built strength in the dark.

Now you're learning how to feel safe again
without needing to look over your shoulder.

That takes time.
The body remembers what the mind tries to forget.
It waits for proof that it can relax,
that this moment won't turn into another disaster.

That proof comes slowly—
in the sound of laughter you don't flinch at,
in the softness of your own breath,
in realizing you went a whole morning
without your chest tightening for no reason.

That's not luck.
That's healing in disguise.

Safety doesn't mean nothing hurts anymore.
It means the world can touch you
without taking something from you.
It means you trust yourself to handle
what comes next—
not perfectly,
but gracefully.

You deserve that.
You deserve the kind of life
where peace and quiet doesn't scare you.

If today still feels uncertain,
that's okay.
Uncertainty doesn't mean danger anymore.
It's just the world reminding you
that not everything can be predicted—
and maybe that's what makes peace possible again.

You don't have to believe it all at once.
You just have to let the quiet stay,
long enough for your heart to notice
that it's safe here.

Because it is.
Right now, in this small moment,
you are safe.

With you in quiet that finally feels safe,
Delilah

Letter Thirteen: Carrying the Simple Things

Dear Sleepless One,

There comes a point
when life starts to fill itself back in.
Not all at once,
not with big announcements—
just quietly,
through the smallest details.

You catch yourself doing something
you haven't done in a long time:
folding towels while a song plays in the background,
stirring a pot and singing along,
answering a text without needing to draft your reply twice.

It doesn't mean the pain is gone.
It means the world has started making space for you again.

At first, you almost don't trust it.
The ease feels too light,
too temporary.
You wait for the heaviness to return
the way it always does.

But even when it does,
it doesn't stay as long anymore.
It visits,
lingers,
and leaves.

And in between its visits,
something softer has taken root.

You might not call it healing.

Maybe it's just endurance.
Maybe it's the body's way of proving
it still knows how to live.

You've spent so much time
rebuilding the strength to survive
that it's strange to realize
you're also learning to live again.

Ordinary moments used to feel unbearable.
Now they whisper reminders
that you're still capable of joy—
not loud joy,
not the kind that needs to be shared,
just quiet joy
that fits inside a single breath.

You don't have to plan your days yet.
You don't have to chase happiness.
You can let life come back to you slowly,
the way light seeps through closed curtains.

It doesn't rush in: it lingers at the edges first,
Barely reaching you-
A faint reminder that warmth still exists.
But slowly, the world starts to soften around you again.
That's how healing begins-
Quietly, in small unnoticed ways.

One morning,
you'll realize you went hours
without thinking of the ache.

You'll notice it only when it returns,
and for a second,
you'll feel guilty.

But that's okay too.
Absence is part of healing.

Your mind needs breaks
from what your heart still remembers.

The truth is—
you're not losing your love.
You're just learning to live around it.

You're allowed to let the world hold you again.
You're allowed to laugh,
to dance,
to say yes to simple things
without explaining where your joy comes from.

You don't have to earn the right to feel okay.
You just have to keep showing up
for the moments that find you.

Ordinary life doesn't erase what came before it.
It simply gives you something new to hold
so the past doesn't have to hold you alone.

Let it.
Let the ordinary come back,
one slow, gentle day at a time.

With you in the moments where joy quietly returns,
Delilah

Letter Fourteen: Steady Again

Dear Sleepless One,

There's moments that arrives quietly, almost without your permission.
You notice it in small ways first—
a message you answer the same day,
a conversation you don't cut short,
a plan you don't cancel at the last minute.

It isn't because everything is better.
It's because something inside you has loosened its grip,
enough to let a little light through the door.

For a long time, connection felt like too much.
Talking cost energy you didn't have.
Smiling felt like a task.
Even happiness could feel sharp against tender soul.

You weren't avoiding people because you didn't care.
You were protecting the parts of you
that were still learning how to breathe.

Now the cuts aren't as deep.
They can still ache,
but they don't split open every time someone asks, *How are you?*
You still don't have an easy answer,
and you don't need one.
Being here is the answer.

You might meet someone's eyes a second longer.
You might tell the truth without telling the whole story.
You might laugh and be surprised that it didn't echo with guilt.

This is how connection returns—
not as a crowd,
but as moments that feel safe enough to keep.

There will be days when the world feels close
and days when it feels far again.
That's not a failure to connect;
it's a body honoring its limits.

You can love people and still need space.
You can want company
and still feel quiet when it arrives.
You can sit across from someone
and say almost nothing
and let that count.

Sometimes you'll feel yourself holding back.
Not because you don't trust the person,
but because you're relearning how to trust your own voice.
It's okay if words take the long way out.
It's okay if your stories come in fragments.
It's okay if you share a single sentence and leave it there.

You once were an open book.
Now you've learned that you no longer
have to be an open book required to explain yourself.
You are a person who has carried enough,
choosing what your heart can afford to offer today.

You'll notice connection in practical places, too—
accepting help without an apology,
saying yes to long drives,
answering *"Is there anything you need?"*
with something real.

It can feel strange at first.
Receiving attention when you've been the steady one,
letting hands carry what yours have carried alone.
But support doesn't erase strength;
it rests it.

There's another kind of connection that returns softly:
the one with your own life.

You catch yourself caring again about small choices—
which mug you use,
which song plays in the car,
which sweater feels like comfort.
They're tiny, forgettable decisions to anyone else,
but to you they're proof that preference has returned,
that you still have a say in how the day fits you.

These are stitches—
not visible from far away,
but they hold everything together.

You may worry what others expect from you now.
Whether they want the "old you,"
or the version who always answers,
or the one who never says no.

You don't have to become any version of yourself
that doesn't feel honest anymore.
Connection that requires performance isn't connection;
it's a costume.
Let yourself outgrow it.

What remains are the people and places
that make room for the person you are now—
quieter in some ways,
clearer in others,
gentle with the time it takes to be human.

If your calendar starts to collect small plans,
it's okay to keep them small.
Coffee that lasts thirty minutes.
A walk that ends when the street turns.
A call that stops before the story does.

You are allowed to leave while you still feel steady.
You don't have to prove you can stay longer than you should.
Real connection respects the point where calm ends.

There will be surprises.
A stranger's kindness that lands exactly where it's needed.
Family who returns without needing the old world back.
A new person who doesn't know your history
and still treats you with the softness it deserves.

Let surprises be surprises.
They don't have to mean more than they do.
They can be an hour that felt easy,
a conversation that didn't drain you,
a reminder that the world still knows how to meet you gently.

If loneliness visits in the middle of connection—
and it might—
that doesn't mean you are doing this wrong.
Loneliness is not cured by proximity;
it eases with time, trust, and the right kind of quiet.
You're allowed to feel the distance
even while sitting beside someone.
You're allowed to leave that feeling unnamed
and let it soften on its own.

One day, without planning to,
you'll realize you reached for your phone
to share something small—
a sky worth noticing,
a joke no one else will understand,
a thought that felt lighter when spoken.

You won't analyze whether it's a sign of progress.
You won't compare yourself to yesterday.
You'll just share it,
and the world will answer back in some simple way,
and that will be enough.

Connection doesn't mean the pain is over.
It means you've made space for more than pain.
It means your life has stretched around loss
and found places where light can live again.

If today those places are few,
that's still plenty.
If they're smaller than you hoped,
they're still real.

This is how it begins:
not with certainty,
but with willingness—
to show up for a moment,
to accept a kindness,
to be seen without having to be understood.

When connection feels possible again,
you don't have to hold it tightly.
You can let it sit near you,
uncomplicated,
the way warm air fills a room.

And when the day ends,
if all that happened was a single easy exchange,
that's more than yesterday had.
That's something the night cannot take.

You're allowed to let it be enough.

With you as life begins to feel like yours again,
Delilah

Letter Fifteen: When Hope Feels Fragile

Dear Sleepless One,

Hope doesn't always arrive like people say it will.
It's rarely bright or loud.
It doesn't always come dressed in promise.
Sometimes it drifts in quietly,
like a draft through a cracked window—
barely noticeable until it brushes your skin.

It doesn't ask for attention.
It just waits to see if you'll notice it.

After everything you've lived through,
hope might not feel safe to hold.
It used to mean believing things would work out.
Now it feels like a gamble—
something you might lose again.

You've learned to protect your heart
by expecting less.
You've taught yourself that disappointment hurts less
when you see it coming.
And maybe you're not ready to let go of that lesson yet.
That's okay.

You don't have to call it hope.
You can call it something smaller—
a possibility,
a pause,
a breath that feels easier than yesterday's.

Hope can be quiet.
It can be cautious.
It can coexist with exhaustion.

It doesn't have to mean
you're ready to rebuild everything.
It just means that somewhere inside you,
there's still a part that hasn't given up entirely.

That's enough.

You might not recognize it at first.
It might show up disguised as curiosity—
in wondering how next week might look,
in noticing the color of the sky again,
in thinking about something other than loss.

That small flicker doesn't erase the pain.
It just reminds you that your story
isn't finished where it broke.

You've carried so much heaviness
that light can feel foreign.
You might even resist it,
as if allowing warmth
means betraying what was lost.

But hope doesn't erase love or memory.
It honors them—
by saying they mattered enough
to keep you reaching for more life.

You don't need to chase it.
You don't need to make it grow.
You just have to let it stay
for as long as it wants.

Sometimes, hope is nothing more
than the decision to see tomorrow
as a possibility,
not a threat.

And if tonight,
all you can manage is a faint curiosity
about what the morning might feel like,
that's still hope—
soft, human, and enough.

With you in the unknown road ahead,
Delilah

Letter Sixteen: The Slow Return of Joy

Dear Sleepless One,

Joy doesn't rush back.
It moves carefully—
like it's tasting your dinner before you serve others.

It shows up quietly,
in the small spaces you almost overlook.
The sound of rain on the window.
The warmth of a drink between your palms.
A laugh that escapes before you realize it's yours.

It's not the kind of joy that shouts.
It doesn't erase the ache.
It simply sits beside it—
soft, patient, real.

For a long time,
you lived without expecting joy.
You stopped reaching for it,
because everything you touched kept slipping away.
You learned to survive in grayscale,
to make peace with the muted tones of endurance.

And then one morning,
without warning,
color begins to bleed back into the edges.
You notice it in the way the light hits the floor.
In the moment you laugh to yourself without meaning to.
In realizing you didn't wake up afraid.

That's joy—
returning in its simplest form.

At first, it feels wrong to feel better.
As if happiness is a betrayal.
As if smiling means forgetting.

But it doesn't.
Joy isn't disloyal.
It doesn't take anything from what you lost.
It honors it—
because you're still here to feel it.

You can hold both things at once:
the ache and the warmth,
the missing and the moment.
That balance is not confusion.
It's healing in motion.

Joy won't stay every day.
It will come and go like weather—
a gentle drift of sunlight through the fog.
But each time it visits,
it will stay a little longer,
and you'll flinch a little less.

You don't have to chase it.
You don't have to explain it.
You just have to let it be what it is:
proof that even after everything,
your heart still knows how to feel light.

And that's not forgetting.
That's surviving beautifully.

With you in the quiet that still breathes with memory,
Delilah

Letter Seventeen: What Was and What's Next

Dear Sleepless One,

There's a quiet season
where nothing feels certain.
Where what you've lost is behind you,
but what's ahead hasn't taken shape.

You're not stuck.
You're simply in the middle.

This is the part nobody talks about—
the stillness that follows survival.
The pause between endings and beginnings.

It feels strange to live in the middle of something
that doesn't have a name yet.

You've spent so long reacting—
holding things together,
carrying what no one saw,
bracing for whatever came next.

Now the quiet feels too loud.
You don't know what to fill it with.
You wonder if this is all that's left.

It isn't.
This stillness is a rebuilding disguised as waiting.
It's where your mind learns peace
and your body learns safety.

You may not see progress here,
but it's happening.
It's in the way your breath steadies faster after crying.

In how you answer messages again.
In how silence doesn't hurt as sharply as before.

This is how healing hides—
in pauses,
in slow days,
in moments you dismiss as nothing.

But they are everything.

You don't owe this part an explanation.
You don't have to define who you're becoming.
You just have to let the middle exist.

The middle is uncomfortable
because it's unfamiliar,
not because it's wrong.

You're not failing to move forward.
You're learning to live without rushing.

One day, this season will end.
You'll walk out of it quietly,
and only later realize
it's what made you whole again.

With you in the moments of the unfamiliar,
Delilah

Letter Eighteen: Believe You Can

Dear Sleepless One,

For a long time,
you lived in survival mode.

Ready for the next loss.
Ready for the next storm.
Ready for the world to ask more than you could give.

You learned how to keep one foot in and one foot out—
a kind of safety that cost you peace.

But now, slowly,
something inside you is loosening.
The ground doesn't feel like a trap.
The days don't feel like a test.

You're learning what it means to have grace.

Grace isn't about never having hard days.
It's about letting yourself belong where you are.
It's about trusting this moment enough
to be in it fully—
not looking back,
not looking ahead,
just here.

You might not call it comfort yet.
Maybe it's only calm.
But calm counts.

It's the first sign
that the world can touch you again
without breaking something open.

There's a kind of courage in showing yourself grace.
In letting time pass without trying to escape it.
In deciding that your presence
is enough reason for the moment to matter.

It's okay if you still brace sometimes.
It's okay if old fear lingers in the corners.
But notice this:
you're not scared anymore.
You're standing still—
and the earth hasn't fallen apart beneath you.

That's proof of change.

You can breathe here.
You can rest here.
You can let the hours unfold
without needing to earn them.

This is what arrival feels like.
Not loud.
Not final.
Just steady.

And one day, you'll realize
you've built a life that doesn't scare you anymore.

That's when you'll know—
you didn't just survive.
You stayed.

And staying was everything.

You used to measure peace by how quiet things were.
Now, its by how safe you feel in the quiet.

With you in learning to give yourself grace,
Delilah

Letter Nineteen: A Soft Kind of Living

Dear Sleepless One,

There are days that don't announce themselves.
They arrive plain and quiet,
the way normal used to.

You move through them without rehearsing each step.
You answer a message.
You make a choice without second-guessing.
You laugh at something small
and it doesn't echo with apology.

Nothing big happens.
That's the point.

For a long time, normal felt out of reach—
a language you used to speak
but couldn't remember anymore.
You translated everything into survival.
You measured hours in effort,
not ease.

So when a day asks less of you,
it can be confusing.
You wait for the hidden cost.
You scan the horizon for a reason
this calm shouldn't count.

But it counts.
In more ways than you can see right now.

This gentle rhythm doesn't mean you've forgotten.
It doesn't mean the past stopped mattering.
It means your life has made enough room
for more than one feeling at a time.

You can miss what is gone
and still enjoy what remains.
You can remember the hard parts
without drowning in them.
You can walk through a store,
hear a familiar song,
and keep your footing when the memory lands.

That steadiness is new.
New doesn't have to be suspect.

There will be a pull to evaluate it.
To ask if you're moving on too quickly,
or not quickly enough.
To label the day so you know where to file it:
good, bad, progress, setback.

But days don't need labels to be real.
They happen, you live them,
and they end.
That has always been true,
even when the hours felt endless.

You may still feel the quiet tighten once or twice—
a knot in the throat,
a pause that stops you mid-motion.
This quiet balance can carry a shadow.
It doesn't cancel itself out because of it.

Shadows mean there is light somewhere nearby.
You don't have to chase it,
and you don't have to turn away.
You can let both exist,
the brightness and the outline it makes.

There's a tenderness to simple tasks now.
Folding towels.
Replying, *Yes, I'm free.*
Choosing your favorite mug because it fits your hand.
These aren't proof that pain is gone.

They're proof that pain isn't the only voice in the room.

You once believed normal would return loudly—
that you'd wake one morning and feel like your old self.
But almost-normal slips in softly.
It settles into habits,
lives inside small choices,
asks nothing dramatic in return.

Sometimes guilt arrives with it.
As if feeling steady means betraying what broke you.
As if ease is a luxury you haven't earned.

Guilt is loud.
Let it talk itself out.
You don't need to argue.
You know what the day cost to reach you.
You know how many nights stood between then and now.
Ease can be honest even when guilt isn't ready for it.

People might not notice the difference.
From the outside, this day looks like any other.
But you know.
You feel the way the room doesn't tilt,
the way the calendar doesn't threaten,
the way your chest doesn't armor itself at noon.

Recognition is private.
You don't have to share it.
You can keep this for yourself:
proof that your system remembers how to live
without a siren in the background.

You don't have to make promises to keep it.
You don't have to decide what tomorrow should be.
You don't have to capture the feeling
or turn it into a lesson.

You can let the day finish
the way it started—
plain and quiet,
useful because it asked so little.

If the evening brings a dip,
that doesn't erase what came before.
A good hour doesn't become a lie
because a hard one followed.
Both happened.
Both count.
Both belong to a life that is wide enough
to hold them side by side.

This quiet balance reveals something you might have doubted:
your capacity.
Not the dramatic kind that lifts cars,
but the everyday kind that carries groceries and conversation,
that answers the door without rehearsal,
that remembers a joke later and smiles at the timing.

Capacity returns like strength after an illness—
quietly, incrementally,
so gradually you argue with it even as you feel it.
You pick up a little more weight than yesterday.
You set it down and realize you could lift it again.

There will be days that don't make it this far.
Days that ask for your bed,
for silence,
for as few decisions as possible.
They are not failures of normal.
They are part of it.
A real life is not a straight line.

This gentle new rhythm doesn't arrive to replace you.
It arrives to meet you where you are.
It takes your hand without insisting you stand.
It sits with you when sitting is the truest thing.

You can trust a day like this
without demanding it to repeat itself.
You can let it be enough
without turning it into proof that you're "better."

Better is a moving target.
Enough is here,
right now,
measured in the soft way time passes
without scraping your skin.

When the night comes,
you may look back and wonder
how something so plain could feel so meaningful.
It's because ordinary is a privilege after chaos.
It's because quiet was once impossible.
It's because this day did not ask you
to explain your existence to it.

You showed up,
and it met you—
no test,
no terms,
no tally to settle at the end.

If tomorrow is harder,
today will still have happened.
It doesn't vanish.
It doesn't shrink.
It sits in memory like a small light
you can see from a distance—
steady, familiar,
a reminder that the road includes this, too.

Not triumph.
Not climax.
Just the soft relief of an almost-normal day,
real enough to rest inside,
honest enough to end
without asking for anything more.

And that is plenty.

With you through days that don't need labels to be real,
Delilah

Letter Twenty: Familiar Ease

Dear Sleepless One,

There was a time
when resting felt impossible.
Your body could be still,
but your mind never stopped running—
through what-ifs,
through what's lost,
through every version of peace you couldn't trust.

You slept with one ear open.
You braced even in silence.
You called it "rest,"
but it was just exhaustion in disguise.

Real rest is different.
It doesn't ask you to perform.
It doesn't need proof that you've earned it.
It meets you where you are—
tired, tense, and human.

It takes practice to believe you can lay down your guard.
To let the world turn without you steering.
To let the air exist without asking what it might carry next.

But it happens slowly.
One night you fall asleep without replaying everything.
One morning you wake
and realize the world went on just fine while you were still.

That's not neglect.
That's peace reclaiming its place.

You may not call it peace yet.
Maybe it's only quiet.

Maybe it's just the absence of panic.
That's enough.

The body remembers chaos longer than the mind does.
It takes time for your muscles to learn
that not every still moment hides a threat.

So if you find yourself tense when nothing's wrong,
be gentle.
That tension is just your old life
checking to see if it's still needed.
You can let it go,
bit by bit.

Rest isn't weakness.
It's the pause that keeps you from collapsing.
It's the reminder that you deserve care
even when no one's watching.
It's the proof that survival isn't meant to be permanent mode—
it's meant to lead somewhere softer.

When rest finally feels safe,
it won't arrive with validation.
It'll come on an ordinary afternoon
when you sit down,
close your eyes,
and realize your body isn't fighting you anymore.

That moment—
that release—
isn't small.
It's sacred.

You've carried too much for too long.
Rest doesn't erase that.
It simply says:
You can stop carrying for a little while.
The world won't fall apart if you breathe.
You won't disappear if you stop trying.

You're allowed to let the silence hold you.
You're allowed to feel safe inside stillness again.

And when you wake,
you'll realize that nothing broke while you rested—
not the world,
not your strength,
and not you.

With you in the stillness,
Delilah

Letter Twenty-One: Learning to Exhale

Dear Sleepless One,

There's a point you reach
where the waiting finally quiets.
You don't notice it at first.
It's subtle—like realizing the house has gone still
after years of alarms.

You've lived so long expecting the next hit,
the next loss,
the next wave that would undo the progress you made.
Your nervous system learned to look for storms
even when the sky stayed clear.

And for a while, that vigilance felt like safety.
It meant you'd be ready next time.
It meant nothing could catch you off guard again.

But it also meant you never truly rested.
You lived in defense of a future
that hadn't even arrived.

One day,
you wake up and realize you're not scanning the horizon anymore.
You're not rehearsing your reactions.
You're just breathing.
And for the first time,
the air feels like yours.

That's not forgetting what happened.
It's recognizing that not every moment
needs to be filtered through fear.

You can stop watching the door.
You can stop sleeping in armor.
You can stop waiting for the next heartbreak
as if anticipation will make it hurt less.

It won't.
It never did.
All it ever did was steal the softness
from the seconds that were safe.

Safety doesn't mean life will never hurt again.
It means you've learned
that pain won't take everything this time.
That you have tools now.
That you have proof you'll find your way back.

You survived the hardest parts
without the certainty you'd make it.
Now, even in uncertainty,
you carry quiet evidence that you can.

There's freedom in no longer flinching at peace.
In not assuming peace is bait.
In learning that quiet can stay quiet
without a catch.

That's the beauty of this stage—
it's not about trusting the world again.
It's about trusting *yourself* in it.
Knowing that even if the next hard thing does come,
you'll still be standing.

You don't have to keep looking for pain.
You don't owe your past
that kind of devotion.

You can let safety be safe.
You can let peace stay.
You can let your body unclench
without wondering when it'll have to tighten again.

It takes time to stop waiting for what broke you.
And it takes bravery to believe
you deserve the ease that's replaced it.

But tonight—
you do.

You've earned the right to exhale
without apology.
To let this moment stand on its own
without bracing for the next one.

Because not every quiet ends in chaos.
Some just stay quiet.
And that,
after everything you've endured,
is its own kind of miracle.

With you in the uncertainty,
Delilah

Letter Twenty-Two: Not Broken Beyond Repair

Dear Sleepless One,

It doesn't happen in a dramatic way.
There's no grand reveal,
no audience clapping for your healing.
It's quieter than that—
so quiet you almost miss it.

One morning,
you catch your reflection
and don't look away.
Not to analyze.
Not to search for the cracks.
Just to notice.

You see someone who has carried too much
and somehow still looks like herself.
A little softer, maybe.
A little wiser.
But still here.

And for the first time,
the word *broken* doesn't fit anymore.

You used to use that word
to explain everything.
The silence.
The fatigue.
The way you couldn't find joy
in places that once held it easily.

You called yourself broken
because the world felt safer
when there was a label for the ache.
Because maybe if you were broken,
you could be fixed.

But what you've done since then
isn't fixing.
It's becoming.

Brokenness implies pieces.
You didn't put pieces back together.
You built something entirely new.

You learned how to live inside loss
without letting it define every corner.
You learned that healing
isn't about going back—
it's about going forward differently.

You still carry scars, yes,
but they don't sting like they used to.
They've become reminders—
of the fires you walked through,
the nights you didn't give up,
the softness you chose
even when the world gave you reasons to harden.

You are not broken.
You're proof that survival can make beauty
out of ruin.

You're evidence
that a heart can be both heavy and whole.
That pain can coexist with peace.
That grief can live beside growth
without taking center stage.

There will still be hard days.
Days that make you question
how far you've really come.
But notice how quickly you return now.
How the spiral doesn't drag you under as long.
How you know where the light switch is
even when it's dark.

That's not luck.
That's strength.
The quiet kind that grows
while no one's watching.

You no longer need to prove your worth
by your wounds.
You no longer need to perform your pain
to be understood.
You can exist without explanation.
You can breathe without apologizing
for how you got here.

That is wholeness.
Not perfection.
Not completion.
Just the peace of knowing
you're living from the center
instead of the fracture.

You are not who you were before the breaking.
You're something far more beautiful,
Inside and out.
More real.
More alive than ever.

And maybe—
that was the point all along.

With you in the wholeness,
Delilah

Letter Twenty-Three: The World Is Yours

Dear Sleepless One,

It happens so slowly
you almost don't notice it.

The days begin to stretch.
The edges that once closed in
start to soften.
You catch yourself noticing things again—
the color of the sky,
the way wind moves through the trees,
the rhythm of traffic in the distance.

The world that felt too loud,
too demanding,
too cruel—
has started to feel open again.

Not because it changed,
but because you did.

There was a time
when everything outside your walls felt threatening.
Too bright.
Too fast.
Too full of other people's ease.

You built a smaller life to survive.
A world within reach,
quiet enough to manage.
It wasn't failure;
it was safety.

But safety can become confinement
when healing begins.

And lately,
you've been peeking over the edges.

You linger outside a little longer.
You walk farther than you meant to.
You talk to someone new and realize
you didn't flinch when they smiled back.

You're not rushing into a new life—
you're expanding into it,
inch by inch,
moment by moment.

There's no urgency now.
No need to replace what's gone.
Just an awareness
that there's more waiting for you
than pain.

The world won't always meet you gently.
But you have learned how to meet it differently.
You listen slower.
You speak with care.
You leave when peace asks you to.

That is not withdrawal—
that's wisdom.
That's knowing how much of yourself
the world gets to hold at once.

Some days,
the old fear might whisper,
"This is too much."
You'll feel your body tense,
ready to retreat.

It's okay.

You can still step back when you need to.
You don't have to prove your courage
by staying in places that drain you.

Expansion isn't a race.
It's a rhythm.
Some days you open wide.
Some days you breathe smaller.
Both are living.

This widening—
this return to curiosity—
isn't about leaving your grief behind.
It's about carrying it differently.
Letting it walk beside you
instead of leading the way.

And the more you move through the world,
the more you'll realize:
you didn't lose your capacity for wonder.
It was just waiting
for you to feel safe enough
to look up again.

So if today you step outside
and the air feels bigger,
don't question it.
Don't rush to understand it.
Just let it hold you.

Because this—
this quiet widening—
is the world saying,
"I never stopped being here."

And you, finally,
are ready to answer back.

With you in the warmth of the sunshine,
Delilah

Letter Twenty-Four: Dreaming Again

Dear Sleepless One,

It begins quietly.
A thought you didn't expect.
A small vision of something that hasn't happened yet—
and for the first time in a long while,
it doesn't scare you.

You've spent years inside survival.
Planning was a luxury you couldn't afford.
Every step felt borrowed,
every hope felt dangerous.
Dreaming required trust,
and trust was the first thing grief took from you.

But now,
something has shifted.
The air feels lighter.
You've begun to imagine again.

You're not building castles in the sky.
You're sketching blueprints for peace.
For possibility.
For the version of you
who doesn't live entirely inside the past.

These aren't grand dreams.
They're small and believable.
A place you'd like to visit.
A project you might finish.
Peace you could allow yourself to look forward to.

And even that—
the act of looking forward—
is a quiet miracle.

You may still hesitate.
Dreams feel fragile after loss.
They remind you of everything
that once fell apart.
You want to hold them loosely,
so they can't break you if they slip away.

But maybe that's not the point anymore.
Maybe dreams were never meant to guarantee outcomes.
Maybe they're simply invitations—
ways of telling yourself,
"I still believe in the possibility of more."

That belief is enough.

You don't need to rush to make them real.
You don't have to turn every idea into action.
Sometimes, the dream itself is what saves you—
the gentle reminder
that your heart still has vision,
even after everything it's seen.

The fact that you can picture tomorrow
means some part of you has already forgiven today.
That's what healing looks like in its truest form.

Not every dream will come true.
But that doesn't make them meaningless.
They're proof of your endurance.
Proof that you still believe
something beautiful can grow
from what broke you.

So if tonight,
you find yourself imagining again—
a new beginning,
a peace you've never known,
a version of you that smiles more easily—
don't silence it.

Let it breathe.
Let it stay.
Let it whisper what's possible.

You don't owe the world realism.
You owe yourself wonder.
And if dreaming is the only thing you can do right now,
then it's enough.

Because every dream that begins at 3 AM
is a quiet promise—
that even after all you've endured,
you still believe in light.

And that belief
is how every new life begins.

With you in dreaming of possibilities,
Delilah

Letter Twenty-Five: When Ease Returns

Dear Sleepless One,

For so long,
tomorrow was something you avoided thinking about.
It felt like a stranger—
too unpredictable,
too fragile,
too easily taken away.

You lived inside the day you were in,
one breath, one task, one quiet survival at a time.
It wasn't weakness.
It was wisdom.
Your body knew you couldn't hold the whole horizon yet.

But lately,
something has changed.

You've caught yourself saying "next week"
without flinching.
You've made small plans—
and meant them.
You've imagined next year
and felt curiosity instead of fear.

That's new.
That's progress disguised as calm.

The future no longer feels like punishment.
It feels like possibility.
Like something you might actually get to see.

You still move carefully.
You still test the air before you trust it.

But you're no longer hiding from what's ahead.

That's how healing introduces itself—
not with clarity,
but with curiosity.

There was a time when you stopped believing
you had any control over what came next.
When every plan dissolved into loss,
and every attempt at hope felt naïve.

You learned to expect the floor to give out.
And when it didn't,
you still braced anyway.

But even fear grows tired.
It can't live at full volume forever.
Eventually, it fades,
and in its place,
you find a cautious kind of wonder.

You don't have to map everything now.
You don't have to decide who you'll be
a year or a decade from today.

You can let the future arrive naturally,
without forcing it into shape.

The truth is—
you're already living pieces of it.
Every time you choose rest over guilt.
Every time you speak gently to yourself.
Every time you let laughter return
without needing permission.

The future isn't waiting for you out there.
It's forming right here,
in the quiet decisions you make daily
to stay,
to try,

to keep your heart open a little longer.

One day,
you'll look around and realize
you stopped surviving your story
and started living it.
You'll notice the absence of dread,
the presence of small ease,
and the surprising thought—
maybe I'll be okay after all.

That's when you'll know
the future no longer feels far away.
It's already arrived.
And somehow,
you made it here.

With you in the understanding,
Delilah

Letter Twenty-Six: Letting the Light In

Dear Sleepless One,

It doesn't happen all at once.
You don't wake up one morning
and find the world transformed.
But one day,
you step outside
and realize the light feels different.

It's not as harsh.
Not as heavy.
It moves softer against your skin—
and for the first time in a long while,
you don't shrink from it.

You let it touch you.

The light hasn't changed, really.
You have.

For months, maybe years,
you looked at brightness as something distant.
Something for other people.
Something you could admire but not belong to.

Now, you stand in it.
Not because the pain has vanished,
but because you've learned
that grief and light
can exist in the same breath.

That your life doesn't need to be dim
to stay loyal to what you've lost.

The world has been quietly waiting
for you to look up again.
And here you are—
eyes open,
shoulders lower,
breathing a little steadier.

It's okay if it feels strange.
It's okay if part of you still doesn't trust it.
After everything,
light can look suspicious at first.
It reminds you of what it felt like to hope,
and hope used to hurt.

But not every beam breaks you.
Some are meant to warm you
back into yourself.

You don't have to do anything with this moment.
You don't have to capture it,
or name it,
or promise it'll stay.

Just notice it.
The way the air feels lighter.
The way the quiet doesn't echo as painfully.
The way your body feels a little less like defense
and a little more like home.

That noticing is enough.

This is what healing looks like
when it stops needing witnesses.
When it isn't loud or performative.
When it's private and real and entirely yours.

The world didn't stop spinning
while you were rebuilding.
But now, finally,
you're spinning with it again.

And the light—
the same light that once felt cruel—
now feels like invitation.

So let it find you.
Let it rest against your face
without apology.
Let it remind you
that there's still beauty to absorb,
still warmth to receive,
still days waiting to unfold
without fear.

You don't owe the world brightness.
You just have to stop hiding from your own.

With you in the natural glow,
Delilah

Letter Twenty-Seven: Simple Happiness

Dear Sleepless One,

Happiness feels unfamiliar at first.
Almost suspicious.
You catch yourself smiling
and instinctively look around—
as if someone might tell you you're not allowed to.

You've lived so long in survival
that joy feels like an interruption,
something too bright to trust.
You brace for it to vanish,
the way everything else once did.

But this time,
it doesn't.

Happiness doesn't ask you to forget.
It doesn't demand that you erase what happened.
It simply asks to sit beside it.
To share the same table
without competing for space.

You can be grateful for what was
and still glad for what is.
You can love what you lost
and still let light in where the cracks remain.

That's not betrayal.
That's balance.

It's okay if the first few smiles feel borrowed.
It's okay if laughter catches in your throat.

It's okay if part of you whispers, *how dare I?*
That's just the old ache
trying to make sense of this new softness.

You're not doing anything wrong.
You're just remembering
what being alive feels like.

Happiness doesn't arrive all at once.
It tiptoes.
It tests the ground before it settles.
You'll find it in the smallest places—
a meal that tastes good again,
music that moves you,
a sunset that holds your attention long enough to make you breathe
deeper.

You'll think, *oh… there you are.*
And that's how joy reintroduces itself—
not with banners,
but with familiarity.

You might not trust it right away.
You might treat happiness like a guest
you're afraid to host too long.
But it isn't here to replace your grief.
It's here to remind you
that you were never meant to live without contrast.

Light and loss can coexist.
They always will.

When happiness visits,
don't question whether you've earned it.
You did—
through every night you endured,
every tear that taught you patience,
every breath that said, *I'm still here.*

You built this moment.

You made space for it,
even when you didn't believe you could.

You're allowed to laugh again.
You're allowed to feel warmth
without apology.
You're allowed to let something beautiful happen
without waiting for it to fall apart.

Because happiness isn't proof that pain is over.
It's proof that pain didn't win.

So when it comes—
softly, slowly,
without warning—
let it stay.
Let it fill the cracks without covering them.
Let it remind you
that this is what healing sounds like:

not silence,
but laughter echoing through the spaces
where grief used to live alone.

With you in the moments of happiness,
Delilah

Letter Twenty-Eight: Safe in Happiness

Dear Sleepless One,

It's one thing to feel happy again.
It's another to feel safe inside that happiness.

For a long time, every good moment felt fragile—
like glass that could shatter
if you breathed too deeply.
You waited for the interruption,
for the loss that always seemed to follow light.

Happiness had conditions.
It came with fine print and expiration dates.
So you learned not to hold it too tightly.
You smiled carefully,
loved cautiously,
and laughed with an edge of fear
that the universe was keeping score.

But happiness doesn't come to test you.
It comes to stay—
if you'll let it.

And lately,
you've been letting it.

You've started to breathe during the good moments,
instead of holding your breath until they pass.
You've started to notice that laughter doesn't always lead to pain.
That comfort can exist
without a catch.

You've started to believe
that happiness might not leave this time.

There's a softness that comes
when you stop anticipating endings.
A peace that unfolds
when you stop measuring love
by how long it lasts.

Happiness doesn't promise permanence.
But it does promise presence.
It asks you to meet it here—
in this moment,
without flinching.

Because the truth is,
you can't lose what you allow yourself to fully live in.
Even if it fades,
you'll always have known what it felt like to be whole again.

Safety inside happiness
isn't about guarantees.
It's about trust—
in yourself.
In your ability to survive whatever follows.
In your capacity to hold peace
without waiting for it to vanish.

The same strength that kept you alive through the dark
is what makes it possible to rest in the light.
You've earned this ease.
You've earned this calm.
You've earned this right to exhale
without suspicion.

So if tonight feels light,
let it.
If your chest feels open,
don't close it.
If laughter finds you easily,
don't hide from it.

This isn't the universe teasing you.

It's life reminding you
that happiness was never gone—
you were just learning
how to feel safe inside it again.

You've always deserved happiness.
Now, finally,
you believe it too.

And that belief—
that quiet acceptance of goodness—
is the most beautiful peace of all.

With you in the reclaiming,
Delilah

Letter Twenty-Nine: The Return of Grace

Dear Sleepless One,

There was a time
when the word *gratitude* made you flinch.
It felt like something people said
to make grief easier to look at—
a way to wrap pain in a pretty package
so it would sit prettier on the table.

You didn't need lessons in perspective.
You needed space to breathe.
And there's nothing wrong with that.

You weren't ungrateful.
You were just surviving.
And survival doesn't leave much room for thank-yous.

But now, something has shifted.
Gratitude no longer feels like pressure.
It feels like presence.

You find it in small, ordinary things—
a moment of quiet,
a kind message,
the way sunlight moves across your floor.

It's not the loud, performative kind of gratitude.
It's subtle.
It lives in your chest quietly,
without demanding you smile through it.

You're not thankful *for* the pain—
you're thankful you made it through it.

You're not thankful *for* the loss—
you're thankful you still know how to love deeply,
even after it.

This kind of gratitude doesn't erase what hurt you.
It simply reminds you
that hurt didn't end you.

And that realization
is its own kind of healing.

You used to think gratitude meant pretending things were fine.
Now, you know it means noticing
what's still good
even when things aren't.

The way your breath returns.
The way laughter sneaks in.
The way your heart—somehow—keeps showing up
even after everything.

That's gratitude.
Not the kind you post about,
but the kind that rebuilds your relationship with living.

There's no shame in taking your time to find this.
Gratitude that's forced is just another mask.
But when it arrives naturally,
you'll feel it—
a warmth that settles deep,
not because everything is perfect,
but because you're still here.

And maybe that's the quiet truth
you've been circling toward all along:

You don't have to be grateful *for* what broke you.
You can simply be grateful
that you survived the breaking.

That's enough.
That's everything.

With you in being grateful for everything that you survived,
Delilah

Letter Thirty: When Peace Feels Like Home

Dear Sleepless One,

Peace used to feel impossible.
Too far away.
Too quiet to trust.

In the beginning, silence felt like loss.
You'd wake in the middle of the night,
and the stillness would ache.
Every calm moment reminded you
of what wasn't there.
Peace wasn't comfort back then—
it was a mirror of absence.

But now, slowly,
it feels different.

Peace no longer asks you to explain yourself.
It doesn't test your strength.
It doesn't demand your guard to be up
or your heart to be hidden.
It just exists.

It meets you in the mundane—
a warm drink,
a slow morning,
a soft breath you don't have to chase.

You used to crave conversation.
Now you crave quiet.
You used to equate calm with emptiness.
Now you recognize it as full.

Full of your growth.

Full of your effort.
Full of the small, invisible ways
you've returned to yourself.

You don't need to earn this calm.
You already did.
Every time you stayed when you wanted to run.
Every time you spoke softly
to the part of you that didn't believe
you'd ever feel safe again.
Every time you allowed stillness
to coexist with sorrow.

That's what built this peace.
Not the world changing—
you did.

You might still have days
when noise finds you again.
When anxiety rises uninvited,
and chaos taps at your door.

That's okay.
Peace isn't the absence of disruption—
it's the presence of stability,
even when disruption arrives.

You know how to return to calm now.
You've built a way back.

Peace doesn't always announce itself.
Sometimes it's just the moment
you stop explaining your worth.
The night you sleep without replaying conversations.
The morning you look in the mirror
and don't feel the need to justify your reflection.

That's peace too.
Unseen.
Steady.
Yours.

This is home now—
not the place,
but the feeling.
The knowing that even if the world outside is loud,
you have an inner quiet no one can take.

You don't have to guard it every second.
You just have to live in it.
Let it breathe with you.
Let it remind you
that peace isn't what you find—
it's what you become.

With you in coming back home to yourself,
Delilah

Letter Thirty-One: What You Been Building

Dear Sleepless One,

There's a moment—
so small you almost miss it—
when you stop measuring your life
by what you've lost
and start seeing it
for what you've built.

It doesn't come with applause.
There's no crowd, no defining event.
It's just you,
doing something ordinary—
folding laundry,
driving,
making a quiet meal—
and suddenly, you feel it:

you're no longer surviving.
You're living.

You spent so long inside the aftermath
that you didn't notice yourself rebuilding.
Piece by piece,
word by word,
you filled the empty spaces
with something new.

Not a replacement—
a continuation.

You carried yourself through fire
and somehow came out softer.

Not because the pain didn't burn,
but because it refined you.
It stripped away everything that wasn't real,
until only truth remained.

There was a version of you
who didn't think she'd make it this far.
You owe her acknowledgment.
You're the reason you're still here.

You're the one who got out of bed
when it didn't make sense to.
The one who stayed kind
when bitterness would've been easier.
The one who kept believing
there was something worth holding on for—
even when she couldn't see it yet.

You deserve to be seen,
not as who you were,
but as who you *needed* to be
to become who you are now.

You don't owe your past self-perfection.
You owe her peace.
You owe her a life
that doesn't revolve around pain.
You owe her the chance
to rest in what you fought for.

Look at where you stand.
Look at everything you carried
that no one saw.
Look at how much you healed
without recognition or reassurance.

You did that.
You.

You may still feel unsteady sometimes.
You may still question your strength.
But doubt doesn't erase progress.
Wobbling doesn't mean you're back at the start.
It just means you're human—
still growing, still becoming, still real.

You're not behind.
You're exactly where you're meant to be—
in the middle of your own becoming.

So tonight,
before you drift to sleep,
let this truth settle in:

You've come further than you think.
You've survived more than you'll ever say.
And you've created a life
that your past self once only dreamed of reaching.

That's not small.
That's everything.

With you in the sifting,
Delilah

Letter Thirty-Two: Love Yourself at All Cost

Dear Sleepless One,

It's strange at first—
to look at yourself with softness
instead of scrutiny.
To see your reflection
and not start with correction.

You've spent so long being your own critic,
holding yourself to impossible standards
as if perfection could protect you
from more loss.

You learned to measure your worth
by what you could do,
what you could fix,
what you could save.
You built a life out of proving.

But love—the real kind—
doesn't need proof.

There comes a day
when you stop apologizing
for the ways you survived.
When you stop calling your boundaries selfish.
When you stop saying "sorry"
for taking up space
in your own healing.

That's where self-love begins.

Not in mirrors or mantras,
but in quiet permission:
to exist without performing,
to rest without guilt,
to take care of yourself
without explaining why.

You don't have to wait
until you've figured everything out
to treat yourself kindly.
You don't have to earn your own gentleness.

You deserve it simply because you're here—
alive,
learning,
still choosing to show up
when you could've chosen to disappear.

That's worth love.

The world will tell you
that self-love means confidence,
achievement,
boldness.
But sometimes it's simpler.
Sometimes it's just noticing
you no longer speak to yourself
with the same cruelty others once did.

It's closing your eyes
and realizing the voice in your head
has softened.
It's catching your reflection
and not looking away.
It's choosing peace
over punishment.

That's love too.

You've been through enough to know
that love can vanish without warning.
That's why this kind matters—
because it can't be taken.
It lives inside you now,
built from the same quiet strength
that carried you through loss.

You don't have to chase it.
You just have to remember
it was always yours.

So tonight,
let yourself exist without improving.
Let your breath be enough.
Let your body be enough.
Let your story—unpolished, unedited—be enough.

You're not perfect.
You're not supposed to be.
You're human—
and somehow,
that's finally starting to feel like enough too.

With you in the self-love journey,
Delilah

Letter Thirty-Three: Trusting Life Again

Dear Sleepless One,

You didn't lose trust in life all at once.
It happened slowly—
moment by moment,
disappointment by disappointment,
until one day you realized
you were living in defense,
not in belief.

You expected loss before love.
Silence before comfort.
Pain before peace.
It wasn't pessimism—
it was protection.

And it made sense.
Because everything you'd trusted before
had broken.

But here you are now—
alive, breathing, healing—
and there's a quiet truth stirring beneath it all:
you're beginning to trust again.

Not blindly.
Not like before.
But softly.
Gently.
With eyes open and heart cautious,
but not closed.

You don't assume every good thing will vanish.
You don't hold your breath waiting for the next hit.
You've learned that unpredictability
doesn't always mean danger.

Sometimes it just means change.
And you can handle change now.

Trust doesn't return as a grand gesture.
It shows up in small moments—
in the way you pour your coffee without rushing,
in the plans you make without fear they'll fall apart,
in the way you start to speak your truth
without rehearsing how it might be received.

You trust that even if things shift,
you'll shift too.
You trust that loss isn't always ending—
sometimes it's space being made
for something new.

You used to beg for certainty.
Now you settle into possibility.
You let life move
without needing to predict its every turn.
You trust your strength
more than you fear the unknown.

That's the difference.
That's growth.

The truth is—
you don't have to trust life perfectly.
You just have to stop fighting it.
To stop assuming it's against you.
To stop believing that pain is the only thing waiting around the corner.

Because there's peace waiting too.
And laughter.
And connection.
And days that don't need meaning to feel good.

You once thought trusting again
meant forgetting what happened.
It doesn't.

It just means you've decided
your past won't be your only teacher.
You're letting life show you something new.

That's not naïve.
That's brave.

So tonight,
don't rush to control what comes next.
Let life meet you halfway.
Let it surprise you kindly.

Because trusting again
doesn't mean everything will be perfect.
It means you've accepted
that even if it's not—
you'll still be okay.

And that knowing
is what freedom really feels like.

With you in trusting that nobody has you like you have yourself,
Delilah

Letter Thirty-Four: Your Circle, Your Choice

Dear Sleepless One,

You spent so long protecting your heart-
So long that kindness started to feel suspicious.
Every new face came with a warning label:
Be careful. Don't get too close. Don't forget what happened last time.

You weren't being cold—
you were being careful.
Because once, letting people in
cost you everything.
So you built quiet boundaries, and for a while,
they were enough.

After a while, you realize protection and peace aren't the same thing.
Boundaries can keep the wrong people out,
But they can also remind you how much you've outgrown.
You start to see that healing isn't about proving your strength-
It's about learning where to place it.

The best kind of healing is the kind you do alone-
The kind that teaches you your own company isn't loneliness,
Its trust.
Being by yourself doesn't mean you're empty;
It means you finally believe you can hold yourself.

And when you're ready
you'll let people back in-
On your own time, in your own way,

One day, someone will have a conversation with you
and you won't feel the urge to flinch.
Their kindness won't make you wary.
Their presence won't feel like pressure.

And you'll realize— you're not afraid anymore.

It doesn't mean you suddenly trust anyone again.
It means you're no longer handing them the power
to break what you've already rebuilt.

You don't owe the world access.
You don't owe anyone proof that you've healed.
Maybe you'll want company again one day,
Or maybe peace in your own space will be enough.
Either way, its your choice.

Choosing yourself isn't loneliness.
It's loyalty- to the peace and happiness you fought for.
Letting people in again doesn't mean trusting easily;
It means you decide who's earned the right to stand near you.

And if that circle stays small-
Or even if it's only you and your kids-
That's still love.
That's still enough.

With you in the peace you've built,
Delilah

Letter Thirty-Five: Loving Yourself Again

Dear Sleepless One,

It took you years
to realize you weren't unlovable—
you were just tired.
Tired of proving,
of pouring,
of begging for help.

You spent so much of your life
loving others,
you forgot the quiet kind of love—
the one that asks nothing,
the one that lets you rest.

Now, you're learning what that feels like.
It's different than you imagined.
It isn't loud or perfect or glowing.
It's the way you breathe softer these days.
It's the way you let yourself rest
without guilt whispering.
It's the way you no longer punish yourself
for not being further along.

That's self-love.
Not a performance—
It's peace.

You don't wake up every morning
feeling whole.
Some days you still ache.
But you speak to yourself differently now.
You don't call the ache weakness.
You call it being *human.*

You forgive yourself faster.
You feed yourself gentler words.
You stand on your own side
even when the world doesn't.

That's how love becomes safe again—
when it lives inside you,
not outside your reach.

You stopped chasing people to feel seen.
You stopped mistaking attention for care.
You stopped apologizing for needing softness.

You started choosing peace
over punishment.
And piece by piece,
that became the proof—
you were never unlovable.
You were just waiting
to be loved correctly—
by you.

Self-love doesn't always glow.
Sometimes it looks like boundaries.
Sometimes it looks like saying no.
Sometimes it looks like sleeping through the storm
because you finally trust
you'll be okay when you wake.

That's the quiet kind of love.
The kind that doesn't leave.
The kind that stays
even when everything else goes quiet.

With you in the rest that you earned,
Delilah

Letter Thirty-Six: Believe in Yourself

Dear Sleepless One,

You didn't stop trusting the world first—
you stopped trusting *you*.

Grief and people do that.
It convinces you that every choice you made
was the wrong one.
It turns hindsight into punishment.
It teaches you to question every instinct
because one day,
everything fell apart
and you were there to witness it.

So you started doubting your voice.
You started second-guessing your yes,
your no,
your enough.

But here's what's true—
you didn't fail.
You just survived something
you were never meant to carry.

Now, you're learning to listen again.
To that quiet pull inside
that doesn't shout or demand,
but whispers: *this feels right.*

You're learning to honor the pause
before you say yes.

You're learning that peace
is a kind of knowing,
and your body feels it
long before your mind catches up.

That's trust.
The gentle kind.
The one that doesn't need proof
to believe in itself.

There will still be days
when doubt creeps in,
asking if you're strong enough,
ready enough,
healed enough.

But trust doesn't mean never questioning.
It means knowing
you can ask those questions
without abandoning yourself.

It means believing
that no matter what happens,
you'll meet yourself with compassion—
not blame.

There was a time you searched for answers
In everyone else-
Their approval, their comfort, their permission.
Now you pause, breathe, and listen inward.
What you find there is steady ground.

You move slower,
but you move with clarity.
You no longer rush to fix.
You wait to understand.

That's growth.
That's wisdom earned the hard way.

When you trust yourself again,
you stop negotiating your worth.
You stop explaining your boundaries.
You stop letting people talk you out
of what your soul already knows.

You don't need approval to stand tall.
You just need to remember
that your own voice
was always the safest place to land.

So if tonight you doubt yourself,
pause.
Breathe.
Ask quietly, *What do I need right now?*
Then listen.
Really listen.

You've carried yourself through the worst already.
You can trust yourself
to carry you through what comes next.

You don't owe anyone proof.
You just owe yourself belief.

With you in the clarity of wisdom,
Delilah

Letter Thirty-Seven: Peace Without Apology

Dear Sleepless One,

For so long,
you explained your peace like it was a crime.
You softened your voice
so, others wouldn't mistake your stillness for pride.
You downplayed your healing
because you didn't want to make anyone uncomfortable.

You thought peace needed permission.
You thought joy required justification.

But now you know—
it doesn't.

You've spent enough nights
earning your right to breathe easily.
You don't have to explain
why you no longer live in the storm.
You survived it.
That's reason enough.

Peace doesn't make you selfish.
It makes you steady.
It makes you whole.

And you don't need to apologize
for the quiet you built
when the world gave you chaos.

People might still misunderstand you.
They might say you've changed,
that you've grown distant,
that you don't "seem the same" anymore.

They're right—
you don't.

You're not performing your pain for validation.
You're not bleeding for attention.
You're no longer living on the edge of exhaustion
to prove you care.

That's not detachment.
That's healing.

You no longer owe your peace to anyone's comfort.
You don't have to shrink to make others feel at ease.
You don't have to relive your trauma
just to prove it happened.

Peace doesn't erase what broke you.
It just means you stopped letting it speak for you.

This peace you've created
isn't the absence of feeling.
It's the presence of understanding.
It's knowing when to stay silent,
when to rest,
when to walk away
without resentment or guilt.

You're not cold.
You're clear.

And clarity has always been the quieter form of strength.

So if someone tells you
you seem different,
say thank you.
You are.

You worked too hard
to keep explaining your healing
to people still addicted to your pain.

Let your peace speak for itself.
It's not arrogance.
It's arrival.

With you in the peace that doesn't need proving,
Delilah

Letter Thirty-Eight: Acceptance as Freedom

Dear Sleepless One,

Acceptance isn't surrender.
It isn't giving up or giving in.
It's finally loosening your grip
on the version of life
you thought you were supposed to have.

It's the moment you stop fighting reality
and start working with it.
The breath that comes after the storm
when you realize—
you don't have to rebuild it all exactly as it was.

You just have to begin again.

For so long,
you thought acceptance meant forgetting.
Like you had to let go of the love,
the memories,
the meaning.
But that's not true.

You don't erase what happened.
You carry it differently.
You stop dragging it through every tomorrow.

The past doesn't vanish—
it just stops being your compass.

You've spent enough time asking *why*.
Acceptance whispers a different question: *now what?*
Not as a demand,
but as an invitation.

It doesn't rush you.
It doesn't erase the ache.
It simply clears the fog enough
for you to see that what's ahead
isn't all pain.

There's still laughter waiting.
Still quiet joy.
Still small, ordinary moments
that won't take everything from you to feel.

Acceptance doesn't mean you stop caring.
It means you stop trying to change
what's already carved into stone.

You stop reopening wounds
to make sense of them.
You stop measuring your progress
by how often you cry.

You begin to see the beauty
in what still stands—
in what's still yours
after everything you endured.

This is the peace that doesn't perform.
The calm that doesn't need fixing.
The freedom that comes
when you stop chasing closure
and start trusting your own continuation.

You no longer look backward
for the version of you that was lost.
You look around—
and find the one who survived.

That's what acceptance is.
Not permission for what happened,
but release from needing it to make sense.

You can hold the love and the loss.
You can honor the past
without living there.
You can breathe again
without waiting for the next ache to prove
you still remember.

This is where the healing quietly turns to freedom.
Not loud, not final,
but true.

Because you finally understand—
you didn't need the ending to change
to find peace.
You just needed to stop waiting for it to.

With you in the honoring the acceptance,
Delilah

Letter Thirty-Nine: The Present is Enough

Dear Sleepless One,

You used to live in the spaces between—
between what you lost
and what you hoped might return.
Between the ache of memory
and the fear of tomorrow.

The present felt too fragile to stand on.
You kept glancing backward for comfort,
forward for control.
Anywhere but *here*.

Because here hurt.
Here was quiet.
And quiet felt like loneliness.

But now,
something has shifted.

You're not waiting for life to start anymore.
You're in it.

Not the version you planned,
but the one you've made with your own hands—
out of grit,
grace,
and days that didn't seem to mean much
until you noticed they added up.

You pour your morning coffee
and realize the silence isn't heavy anymore.
It's peace.

You watch the sunlight stretch across the floor
and you don't wish to be anywhere else.

That's presence.
That's arrival.

The present used to feel small compared to your dreams.
Now it feels sacred.
It holds all the proof you need—
that somehow, through everything,
you're still becoming.

You no longer need every moment
to be extraordinary.
You just need it to be honest.

You find meaning
in the exhale of your own breath,
in the way time slows when you let it,
in the realization
that life doesn't need to impress you
to be worth loving.

You don't have to chase the next thing anymore.
You don't have to measure your peace
by productivity.
You don't have to rush toward what's next
to justify surviving what's passed.

Being here—
breathing, noticing, feeling—
is enough.

It always was.

This is what healing looks like
when it stops needing a goal.
It's the moment you realize
the miracle was never waiting out there.
It was the way you stayed.

The way you kept showing up
for your own ordinary life
when no one else could see its beauty yet.

You built this moment
from your own stillness.
You made "enough" mean something real.

So if tonight feels quiet,
let it.
You're not missing out on anything.
You're inside it—
the peace you once begged for.

The present is no longer something to survive.
It's something to live inside.
And you, finally,
belong to it.

With you in still standing, still present,
Delilah

Letter Forty: Thank Yourself

Dear Sleepless One,

There are so many people you've thanked along the way—
the ones who showed up,
the ones who said the right words,
the ones who tried in small ways to help you breathe again.

But tonight,
this one's for you.

For the version of you who didn't get flowers.
Who didn't get credit.
Who didn't get help—
but kept going anyway.

The one who cleaned the mess
while her heart was breaking.
Who smiled for her kids
when her soul was trembling.
Who sat in the dark
and somehow still reached for light.

That woman deserves your gratitude.

You've spent years giving compassion away.
Now it's time to turn it inward.
To look at yourself not through judgment,
but through awe.

You've been your own constant.
Your own healer.
Your own witness.
And you did it without applause.

You showed up for a life
that kept asking too much of you—
and still found ways to give it meaning.

That's not luck.
That's love.

Thank yourself
for every morning you rose
when you didn't know how you would.
For every time you refused to harden.
For every day you let the world see your strength
without seeing the war behind it.

Thank yourself
for the patience you learned the slow way.
For the softness you chose
when anger would've been easier.
For the peace you built
from the ruins no one else wanted to touch.

You don't owe yourself perfection.
You owe yourself recognition.
You owe yourself gentleness for every chapter
you endured in silence.

There's a kind of healing
that only comes when you finally say—
thank you, me.

Not as a joke,
not as a whisper,
but as a truth.

Because the truth is,
you're the reason you're still standing.

No one else knows what it took.
No one else saw the private battles you fought.
But you did.

And you stayed.
Even when it didn't feel worth it.
Even when it didn't feel possible.

That deserves gratitude.
That deserves grace.
That deserves rest.

So tonight,
don't rush to thank the world.
Thank the hands that carried you through it.
Thank the heart that kept beating,
even when it was broken.
Thank the woman
who turned her own pain
into proof of what survival looks like.

She saved you.

And she's still saving you,
every day you choose to keep living.

With you in never giving up on yourself,
Delilah

Letter Forty-One: Finding Home Within

Dear Sleepless One,

You spent so long trying to find peace
in other people,
in places,
in plans that kept shifting beneath your feet.

You thought home was something you built outside yourself—
a house, a relationship, a promise, a future.
Something to hold onto
so you wouldn't have to feel the emptiness.

But the truth came quietly.
Home was never a place.
It was always you.

It took years to arrive here—
to the version of yourself
who doesn't need constant fixing,
who can breathe without permission,
who can sit in her own silence
and feel comfort instead of fear.

That's peace.
The steady kind.
The one that sings to your soul
when you finally stop fighting your own reflection.

You've stopped apologizing
for the ways you had to grow.
You've stopped shrinking
to make your strength less visible.
You've stopped searching
for who you were before it all fell apart.

You're not her anymore—
and you don't need to be.

There's something sacred
about realizing you like your own company again.
That you trust your own thoughts.
That you no longer feel the need
to explain your peace and happiness
or justify your boundaries.

You move slower now.
You choose softer words.
You see beauty in moments
you once rushed past.

You've learned how to belong
without losing yourself.

This is what home feels like—
not walls or rooms,
but the feeling that you can rest
anywhere you are.

You've created safety inside your own skin.
You've built peace
from the pieces that were meant to break you.

And that's something so powerful—
a quiet arrival.

So if tonight feels still,
don't reach for noise.
Let the quiet stay.
Let it wrap around you like a warm blanket.

You've made it here—
to the place where your heart
no longer needs to wander.

You are home now.

With you in the remembering your power,
Delilah

Letter Forty-Two: Gently Living

Dear Sleepless One,

For a long time, the world felt sharp.
Every noise startled you.
Every plan felt like a setup.
Even joy carried an edge—
because comfort had betrayed you before.

You moved carefully,
half-expecting life to turn on you again.
You called it caution,
but sometimes it was fear in disguise.

And honestly—who could blame you?
You were rebuilding from ashes.
You were learning to breathe in a place
that once took your breath away.

But lately, something's softened.

You don't brace at every sound anymore.
You don't question every calm day.
You catch yourself smiling
without wondering how long it will last.

That's not carelessness.
That's healing.

You're learning to live gently again—
to meet the world
without flinching.

Gentle living isn't about ignoring pain.
It's about refusing to carry it into every moment.

It's the way you choose slower mornings
and unhurried thoughts.
It's the way you listen before reacting,
the way you give yourself grace
when you forget how far you've come.

You no longer need to force meaning
from every experience.
You just let things be.
Some days heavy,
some days light,
all of them real.

You move differently now—
not from fear,
but from awareness.
You see the world through edges that have softened,
and it meets you with gentleness in return.

You no longer live waiting for disaster.
You live noticing small proofs of peace:
the warmth of your coffee,
a singing your favorite song,
the quiet rhythm of your own breath.

That's enough.

There's strength in this stillness.
In knowing that you can exist fully
without constant tension.
In letting softness be your response
to a world that once made you hard.

You're not naive.
You're free.

Free to walk through life
without armor made of exhaustion.
Free to let joy feel easy
and peace stay simple.

Living gently doesn't mean nothing will hurt again.
It just means you trust yourself
to hold whatever comes next
without breaking.

That's the quiet miracle of it all—
the world didn't get easier.
You just stopped needing to fight it.

And in that surrender,
you finally found ease.

With you in the slower routines,
Delilah

Letter Forty-Three: Belonging Again

Dear Sleepless One,

There was a time
when you felt like a ghost in your own story—
present, but not fully here.
You went through the motions,
did what needed to be done,
and called that living.

But deep down,
you knew you were just existing.
Breathing, but not connected.
Moving, but not feeling.

It wasn't apathy.
It was protection.
You'd been hurt by life one to many times,
and you weren't ready to trust it again.

And then—quietly—something began to change.
You stopped standing on the edges.
You started letting the world touch you again.

Not in big, sweeping ways,
but in small ones.

The sound of laughter in another room.
The warmth of sunlight on your hands.
The pull of a song that made your chest ache
in a good way this time.

The world didn't suddenly get kinder.
You just started letting it in.

Belonging doesn't happen all at once.
It starts with noticing.
It grows through presence.
It expands every time you say,
I'm still here.

Because you are.
And you matter.
Not as a survivor.
Not as a story.
Just as a human being
still learning how to live.

You've spent enough time feeling separate—
like you were watching everyone else move forward
while you stood still.
But the truth is,
you were never behind.
You were just healing.

Now, that healing is starting to trickle quietly
beneath your everyday life.
You belong again—
not to the world you lost,
but to the one you're creating.

You find connection in simple things:
in how the air feels after rain,
in the way people still smile at strangers,
in moments that remind you
life hasn't given up on you,
even when you almost gave up on it.

You're not chasing purpose anymore.
You're living it—
in every gentle decision
to stay open,
to stay soft,
to stay here.

This is belonging.
Not fitting in.
Not performing wholeness.
Just breathing with the world again
instead of holding your breath against it.

You no longer need to prove
you've earned your place in life.
You were never separate from it.

You were just finding your way back.

And now, finally,
you have.

With you in the wholeness,
Delilah

Letter Forty-Four: When Time Softens

Dear Sleepless One,

There was a season when time hurt.
Every sunrise reminded you
of what was missing.
Every milestone felt like a wound
you had to smile through.

You wanted it to move faster—
to hurry you out of the ache.
And yet,
when it did,
you grieved that too.

Because moving forward
felt like leaving something sacred behind.

You were caught between longing and survival,
between holding on and moving forward.
And no matter which you chose,
it hurt.

But time has softened its grip on you.
You don't count days anymore.
You live them.

You no longer chase healing
like it's a race you need to win.
You've learned that it unfolds
in its own quiet rhythm—
and you move with it now,
not against it.

There's peace in that.

You used to fear forgetting.
Now you understand
that remembering doesn't mean reliving.
You can honor what was
without being trapped inside it.

Time didn't take your love away.
It taught you how to carry it differently.

That's what healing really is—
not erasing,
but transforming.

You look at old photos now
and don't fall apart.
You smile.
You remember the sound of a laugh,
the warmth of a hand,
and instead of breaking,
you breathe.

The ache doesn't own you anymore.
It just visits.
And you let it come and go
like weather.

Because you know now—
it always passes.

You've made peace
with the way time moves.
You no longer beg it to rewind.
You no longer fight it for control.
You trust it—
to carry you forward
without stealing what matters.

You've learned that time doesn't heal *you*.
You heal *within* it.

You do the living,
and time simply holds the space.

So tonight,
if you feel that quiet tug between past and present,
don't resist it.
Let it stretch.
Let it hold both truths:
that you've lost,
and you've grown.
That something ended,
and something else began.

You are not running out of time.
You are walking with it.
And for the first time in a long while,
it feels like comfort—
not a countdown.

With you in the softness,
Delilah

Letter Forty-Five: When the Future Feels Safe

Dear Sleepless One,

There was a long stretch of time
when the future felt like a threat.
You stopped making plans
because everything you'd planned once
had fallen apart.

You didn't dream anymore.
You didn't hope too loudly.
You lived in small, careful moments—
afraid that wanting more
might somehow invite loss back in.

It wasn't fear of failure.
It was fear of breaking again.

You thought safety meant standing still.
But stillness began to ache, too.

Now, you're beginning to feel something new—
not excitement exactly,
but openness.
You can think about next month
without bracing.
You can imagine next year
without the old dread creeping in.

That's progress.
That's trust returning.
That's healing quietly doing its work
behind the scenes.

You don't have to plan your life in detail.
You just have to stop hiding from it.

The future doesn't ask you to forget.
It just asks for a small kind of hope—
not in outcomes,
but in *you*.

Hope that you'll meet whatever comes
with the strength you've already proven.
Hope that joy won't destroy you this time.
Hope that you'll know how to rebuild
if things ever break again.

That's the courage you carry now—
not blind optimism,
but steady readiness.

Looking ahead doesn't mean rushing forward.
It just means allowing possibility again.
It's the gentle thought—
maybe there's more for me than what's already happened.

It's saying yes to a day trip
without wondering what could go wrong.
It's leaving room for joy
without demanding guarantees.

You no longer need the future to promise safety.
You've learned how to create safety within yourself.
That means you can look ahead now—
not because life is predictable,
but because *you are steady.*

You can hold what comes next
without losing yourself to it.
You can want again
without fear being the loudest voice.

That's not naïve.
That's brave.
And you've earned it.

So if tonight your thoughts wander forward,
don't pull them back.
Let them dream a little.
Let them imagine peace that lasts,
love that feels easy,
life that feels like living.

Because looking ahead
isn't about replacing the past.
It's about trusting
that you're finally strong enough
to meet what's next—
and to let it be good.

With you in the possibility of tomorrow,
Delilah

Letter Forty-Six: Hope, Gently Returning

Dear Sleepless One,

Hope used to feel heavy.
It was the thing that lifted you—
then dropped you when life shifted again.
Every time you let yourself believe,
something came along to remind you
why believing hurt.

So you taught yourself to live without it.
To stay neutral.
To keep your expectations low
so disappointment couldn't find you.

But living without hope
wasn't peace.
It was protection that slowly turned into numbness.

And numbness isn't living.

Hope is returning now—
not loud,
not dramatic,
but quiet.
It sings beneath the surface of your ordinary days,
showing up in small ways
that don't demand to be noticed.

It's in the way you buy flowers again.
The way you start a list for the future.
The way you catch yourself imagining something good
without cutting the thought short.

That's hope,
coming back on its own terms.

You don't have to announce it.
You don't have to trust it completely.
You just have to let it exist
without shutting the door on it.

This version of hope is gentler.
It doesn't promise that everything will work out.
It just whispers that something might—
and that's enough.

You can hold it softly this time.
You don't have to cling.
You don't have to make it a vow.

Just let it live quietly beside you,
a reminder that maybe,
the worst parts of the story
aren't the only ones left to tell.

You've carried despair.
You've carried exhaustion.
You've carried loss.
You know their weight by heart.

Now, you're learning
that hope has a weight too—
but it's lighter.
And you can carry that, too.

You can let it balance the heaviness,
not replace it,
but exist beside it.

That's what real healing looks like—
not choosing one feeling over another,
but learning how to hold both
without losing your center.

You no longer have to fear hope.
You can trust yourself with it.
You've proven that even when things fall apart,
you don't.

So tonight,
if a small spark flickers in your chest—
don't blow it out.
You've earned it.
Let it stay.

Because hope isn't a promise.
It's an invitation—
to believe that maybe,
just maybe,
there's still more light waiting ahead.

With you in the brighter days ahead,
Delilah

Letter Forty-Seven: Seeing Beauty Again

Dear Sleepless One,

There was a time
when beauty felt cruel.
It reminded you of what was gone—
what used to make your heart happy
before loss rearranged your world.

You looked at sunsets and felt nothing.
You heard music and turned it off.
You saw people laughing
and wondered what it must feel like
to belong to that kind of light again.

Beauty didn't comfort you then.
It mocked you.
Because joy felt like something
you couldn't reach anymore.

But now,
you're starting to notice again.

Not all at once,
and not every day,
but enough to feel it:
that quiet ache of appreciation
that isn't pain—it's presence.

You catch yourself pausing
at the way morning light touches the wall.
You smile at the sound of rain.
You notice a things
you haven't seen in years
and it moves you for no reason at all.

That's beauty returning.
That's life whispering,
"I'm still here."

You don't need to chase it.
It's already around you.
In the small, ordinary things
you used to look past
because survival took all your focus.

Now, survival has softened into living.
And living has opened the door
to wonder again.

It's not loud,
and it's not constant—
but it's real.

Beauty feels different now.
It doesn't demand that you forget.
It lets you remember
without breaking.

You can look at the sky
and think of who you've lost
without collapsing under it.
You can feel warmth
without guilt.
You can let peace and grief
share the same space in your chest.

That's balance.
That's becoming whole again.

You used to think beauty would hurt forever.
But it's not the beauty that hurt.
It was the longing.
The distance between what was
and what still could be.

Now, that distance has closed.
You're not outside your own life anymore.
You're in it.
Feeling it.
Noticing it.

And maybe that's what healing truly is—
not when pain disappears,
but when beauty starts meaning something again.

So tonight,
if something catches your eye—
a flicker of light,
a familiar song,
a quiet moment that moves you for no reason—
don't look away.

That's not the past calling.
That's the present saying,
Welcome back.

With you in seeing the beauty of life again,
Delilah

Letter Forty-Eight: When Here Is Enough

Dear Sleepless One,

You used to wake up
and feel the weight of the day
before you even opened your eyes.
The thought of another sunrise
felt more like endurance
than beginning.

You moved through the hours
because you had to—
not because you wanted to.
Every breath was survival.
Every step was obligation.

You weren't living.
You were lasting.

And that was enough for a while.
It had to be.

But something has changed now.
You can't pinpoint when.
Maybe it was a quiet morning.
Maybe it was a laugh you didn't expect.
Maybe it was nothing at all—
just a slow, gentle shift
that built itself from all the days you stayed.

You woke up one morning
and the air felt lighter.
You realized your chest wasn't tight.
You realized you weren't waiting
for something bad to happen.

You realized—
you were just alive.
And that felt like enough.

It's not that the pain is gone.
It just doesn't lead anymore.
You still carry it,
but it moves differently now—
behind you, not in front of you.

You walk beside it with grace.
You let it belong to your story
without letting it define the chapter you're in.

That's not forgetting.
That's living.

Life feels softer these days.
Not easier,
just more free.
You notice small things again:
how your body feels when it's rested,
how laughter sneaks up on you,
how peace can live quietly
even when everything isn't perfect.

You used to think joy had to be loud.
Now you know it can whisper.
And you still hear it.

You don't have to make your life impressive.
You don't have to prove your resilience.
You don't have to pretend it doesn't still hurt sometimes.

You just have to keep being here.
Showing up.
Choosing to see another day.

Because being alive
isn't the consolation prize.

It's the miracle you almost forgot you were living.

So if tonight is peaceful,
don't rush it away.
Let it sit beside you.
Let it remind you
that you've made it through enough storms
to deserve this ease.

You don't have to chase purpose tonight.
You don't have to fix anything.
You don't have to do anything at all.

Just breathe.
Exist.
Be alive.

That's enough.
And maybe—
that's what peace was always trying to tell you.

With you in the slow return,
Delilah

Letter Forty-Nine: Contentment, At Last

Dear Sleepless One,

You spent years chasing peace—
believing it would arrive
once everything made sense,
once life looked different,
once the ache stopped echoing.

You chased healing like a finish line.
You thought it would come with fanfare,
a moment where everything clicked
and you'd finally feel whole again.

But healing didn't come that way.
It came in fragments.
It came in pauses.
It came quietly,
until one day you realized—
you weren't chasing anymore.

You were simply *here*.

Contentment doesn't announce itself.
It doesn't need to.
It shows up softly—
in the way you stop comparing,
in the way you stop needing to be understood,
in the way you can sit in silence
and not feel like something's missing.

You used to think peace would mean perfection.
Now you know it just means presence.
It's the ability to live inside this moment
without wishing for another one.

That's not settling.
That's arriving.

You've learned to stop grading your life
by the scale of joy versus pain.
You understand now
that both exist,
and both belong.

Contentment is the in-between—
the steady hum beneath it all.
It's what remains
when the highs fade
and the lows quiet.

It's not excitement,
and it's not emptiness.
It's steady.
It's safe.
It's peace that stays.

You don't wake up searching for proof anymore.
You don't measure your worth by how loud your progress sounds.
You move through your days
with gentleness toward yourself,
with forgiveness for what you can't change,
and with gratitude
for what still finds its way to you.

You no longer rush to the next thing
because you've realized—
you already have what you once prayed for:
stability, calm, breath, awareness.

That's not nothing.
That's everything.

So tonight,
when you feel that quiet stillness
settle over your chest,
don't question it.
Don't look for meaning.
Don't wonder how long it will last.

Just rest in it.
Let it be what it is—
not a sign,
not a lesson,
just a moment where you finally feel safe
inside your own life.

You don't have to keep searching.
You're allowed to stay.

This is contentment.
And it found you
the moment you stopped running.

With you in the quiet that needs no more searching,
Delilah

Letter Fifty-One: Trusting Yourself Again

Dear Sleepless One,

You spent a long time being your own backup plan.
Holding yourself together
when no one else knew how.
Doing the hard things quietly,
because you couldn't risk falling apart.

That kind of strength was necessary—
but it came at a cost.
It taught you to survive alone,
and sometimes it made you believe
you always had to.

Now, you're learning a softer way.
You still trust yourself to stand tall,
but you no longer confuse self-reliance
with isolation.

You've proven you can carry the world.
Now it's time to prove
you can also set it down.

Forgiveness begins here—
not for what others did,
but for how hard you were on yourself
when you were just trying to make it through.

You blamed yourself for missing the signs,
for staying too long,
for not knowing better back then.
But you did know something:
you knew how to keep going.
And that was everything.

You don't need to apologize
for who you had to be to survive.
You just need to thank her
for getting you here.

Self-trust isn't about never falling again.
It's about believing you'll rise
without punishing yourself for the stumble.

You don't owe yourself perfection.
You owe yourself compassion.
Because the truth is—
you've already earned it a hundred times over.

Every moment you chose growth instead of guilt,
every time you let a lesson soften you
instead of hardening you,
you rebuilt trust in yourself.
Not through certainty,
but through kindness.

You can lean on you now—
not from fear,
but from peace.
You can love the parts that once made mistakes
without needing to fix them.
You can hold yourself accountable
without withholding grace.

This is what it means to be whole:
to trust yourself
and forgive yourself
in the same breath.

So tonight,
if old regrets try to speak,
let them.
Listen.

And then tell them gently—
I've made peace with her.
She did her best.
And she's finally safe now.

Because you are.

And that's what healing looks like
when it's no longer survival—
but self-acceptance in its purest form.

With you in the gentle steadiness of enough,
Delilah

Letter Fifty-Two: Home Within

Dear Sleepless One,

There was a time
when you lived everywhere but here—
in memories that wouldn't let go,
in dreams you were afraid to touch,
in versions of yourself
you kept trying to fix or become.

You searched for belonging
in people, in purpose, in progress.
And while all of those things mattered,
none of them lasted.
Because the one place you hadn't learned to rest
was inside your own being.

You were always halfway gone—
to the past,
to the next goal,
to the next reason to prove you were okay.

But somewhere along the way,
you stopped running.

You didn't even notice it at first.
You just began to breathe easier in your own company.
You caught your reflection one morning
and didn't rush to critique it.
You realized silence wasn't empty anymore—
it was safe.

This is what arriving feels like.
Not a grand moment.
Not a finish line.

Just a quiet settling into yourself
after years of chasing versions
that were never meant to stay.

Being at home in yourself
doesn't mean you have everything figured out.
It means you no longer abandon who you are
just to be loved or understood.

You can stand in your truth now
without needing to defend it.
You can rest inside your own skin
without wishing for another one.

The peace you were searching for
was never outside of you.
It was waiting
for you to stop searching.

You don't need to reinvent yourself anymore.
You've done enough rebuilding.
Now it's time to live.
To wake up and move through the day
as someone who belongs to herself first—
not out of ego,
but out of care.

It's okay if some days still ache.
It's okay if old versions of you whisper sometimes.
You can listen without leaving yourself to chase them.

That's what home feels like.
It doesn't erase the past.
It just makes room for it
without letting it take over.

So tonight,
breathe in your own steadiness.
You don't have to prove you've healed.
You don't have to apologize for existing fully.

You are your own safe place now.
Not because you stopped needing anyone,
but because you finally came home to you.

And that's where you'll stay—
softly,
bravely,
completely,
enough.

With you in the stillness that finally feels like home,
Delilah

Letter Fifty-Three: Ready to Be Seen

Dear Sleepless One,

For a long time, you kept your light dim.
Not because you didn't have anything to give—
but because the world felt too loud
for a heart still learning to beat softly again.

You grew comfortable in your quiet.
It was safe there.
Predictable.
You could control what came close
and what stayed away.

But now there's a pull—
a gentle stirring that says,
you don't have to hide anymore.

You've spent so much time rebuilding
that you forgot:
you were meant to live out loud, too.

Being seen again isn't about performance.
It's not about pretending you're fine
or proving your strength to anyone.
It's about allowing yourself
to exist in full color—
without shrinking,
without apologizing,
without fear of being misunderstood.

Because being seen
isn't just about visibility.
It's about honesty.

It's about letting the world meet you
as you truly are—
not as who you thought you had to be to survive.

There was a time when being visible felt dangerous.
When vulnerability equaled risk.
When you learned to protect yourself
by disappearing.

But you've grown since then.
You've built boundaries that feel like peace,
not walls.
You've learned how to be open
without losing yourself in the process.

Now, showing up
doesn't feel like exposure.
It feels like arrival.

The world hasn't changed much.
But *you* have.
You move slower.
You speak softer.
And yet, somehow,
your presence carries more weight now—
because it comes from truth.

You don't chase attention.
You attract resonance.
You don't need to convince anyone
of your worth.
You simply *are*.

And when you live that way,
the right people see you.
Not because you shouted,
but because your authenticity whispered—
and they listened.

You can walk into rooms now
without rehearsing who you need to be.
You can speak
without fearing what they'll think.
You can let others witness your becoming
without letting their gaze define it.

Because you finally understand:
being seen is not the same as being exposed.
It's being known.
And being known begins
with knowing yourself.

So if today the world feels like it's calling you out again,
don't shy away.
You're not stepping back into the spotlight.
You're stepping into alignment.

This is what readiness looks like—
not loud,
not polished,
just real.

You've spent enough time hiding.
The world deserves to meet this version of you—
and you deserve to be seen.

With you in the calm that asks for nothing more,
Delilah

Letter Fifty-Four: Letting In What's Safe

Dear Sleepless One,

There was a time
when connection felt like danger.
You'd open your heart halfway
and keep the rest hidden behind careful smiles.
You wanted closeness—
you just didn't trust what it might cost.

You had learned the hard way
that love could hurt,
that people could leave,
that being needed
didn't always mean being valued.

So you made yourself your own anchor.
And it worked.
You stayed steady.
You stayed safe.
But you also stayed alone.

Now you're ready for something different.
Not the kind of connection that drains or defines you—
but the kind that meets you where you are.
You've learned that love, friendship, and care
don't have to mean losing yourself again.

You can open the door without handing over the key.
You can share your softness
without letting it be taken for weakness.
You can give without emptying.
You can receive without guilt.

This is what healthy closeness feels like—
mutual, calm, honest, and present.

The right people won't ask you to shrink.
They'll make space for your fullness.
They'll listen without fixing,
care without controlling,
and stand beside you
without pulling you backward.

You'll recognize them easily.
Not because they're perfect,
but because you feel peace when you're near them.
Not chaos.
Just peace.

That's how you'll know
it's safe to let them in.

You've outgrown relationships built on survival.
You crave the kind that honors growth—
the ones where you can talk about hard things
and still feel respected when it's quiet again.

You no longer chase connections.
You build it from the overflow.
And that changes everything.

So tonight,
if someone reaches for you—
emotionally, kindly, quietly—
don't rush to pull away.
You can open your heart
and still protect your peace.

You can let people in
without losing yourself in the process.
That's not weakness.
That's wisdom.

Because now,
you know the difference
between losing yourself after loss
and finding yourself through it.

With you in the quiet proof that peace can stay,
Delilah

Letter Fifty-Five: When You Start to Trust Life Again

Dear Sleepless One,

There was a stretch of time
when life felt like a test you hadn't studied for.
Every calm moment carried suspicion.
Every new beginning felt like a setup.
You kept waiting for the next heartbreak,
the next loss,
the next wave to undo the little peace you'd found.

You called it caution.
But it was fear—
the kind born from too many endings.

You didn't trust life anymore.
And honestly, how could you?
It had taken too much.

But slowly,
almost quietly,
life began to show you small proofs of safety again.

Not guarantees.
Just moments.

The way laughter came easier one afternoon.
The way you caught yourself planning something for the future.
The way nothing bad happened
when you allowed yourself to feel happy.

That's where trust begins—
in the ordinary.
In the absence of catastrophe.

In the simple truth
that sometimes things really can stay okay.

You've learned that trust doesn't mean blind optimism.
It means choosing not to live in constant defense.
It's soft,
not naïve.
It's the quiet decision
to let life hold you
without fighting its every curve.

You no longer demand promises.
You let the moment be enough.
You let the uncertainty coexist with peace.

Because deep down,
you know that even when everything changes,
you'll still be you—
and you'll still know how to find your way.

You're not waiting for the world to prove it won't hurt you again.
You're building trust in your own resilience—
the way you keep finding meaning
in places that once only brought pain.

You trust yourself
to create light when it goes dark.
You trust time
to reveal what effort alone can't.
You trust that whatever comes next
will not undo what you've become.

Life isn't something to brace against anymore.
It's something to breathe with.
To walk beside.
To learn from, not fear.

You no longer need it to make sense
to know it's still worth living.

You've been broken and rebuilt enough times
to understand that both are part of the rhythm.

So tonight,
let the world turn without resistance.
You're not behind.
You're not cursed.
You're just human—
and you're finally learning to trust life again.

And that?
That's what freedom really feels like.

With you as life begins to feel safe again,
Delilah

Letter Fifty-Six: Let Life Surprise You

Dear Sleepless One,

For so long, you needed to know what was coming next.
You tried to read every sign,
prepare for every outcome,
protect yourself from every possible ache.

It made sense—
you'd lived through enough loss
to understand how quickly things can change.
You thought being ready
would keep you safe.

But all it really did
was keep you braced.

And you can't live fully
with your shoulders always tight.

Now you're learning to loosen your grip—
to let life meet you
instead of trying to outrun it.

You notice that not every silence is a warning.
Not every calm moment is the pause before pain.
Sometimes it's just peace.
Sometimes things go right.
Sometimes the ending isn't tragic—
it's just quiet, gentle, true.

You're realizing
that not every surprise has to hurt.

Letting life surprise, you
means letting go of the need to predict.
It's allowing joy to arrive unannounced.
It's saying yes before fear finds a reason to say no.
It's letting curiosity guide you again—
the kind you thought was lost for good.

You find it in small ways now:
a stranger's kindness,
an unexpected laugh,
a song that reaches the exact part of you
you thought no one could touch anymore.

That's how wonder returns—
softly,
without asking permission.

You don't have to prepare for every outcome.
You don't have to guard against every good thing.
You can let life show up how it wants to—
unpredictable, imperfect,
but still full of beauty you don't have to earn.

Because the truth is—
the best moments never come from control.
They come from openness.

You've survived enough endings
to know you'll be okay,
no matter how the story unfolds.

So now,
you can open your hands again.
You can live in the surprise.

And when something beautiful catches you off guard—
don't question it.
Don't analyze it.
Don't rush to understand why.

Just let it happen.
Let it remind you
that not all change is loss,
and not all surprises are pain.

Sometimes, life still has soft edges.
Sometimes, the unexpected
is exactly what your heart was waiting for.

With you in letting life reveal itself in its own time,
Delilah

Letter Fifty-Seven: When the Spark Returns

Dear Sleepless One,

There was a time
when even simplest things felt heavy.
When your days blurred together and your
mind stayed quiet-
Not peaceful quiet, but survival quiet.
You weren't lazy or uninspired.
You were saving every ounce of energy just to keep going.

Your world had gone quiet,
and for a while,
that silence was a shield.
You needed it.
You needed rest from effort,
from believing,
from disappointment.

But lately, something feels different.
The silence doesn't feel empty anymore.
It feels open.
You start to notice small things again-
the way light moves across a room,
the taste of your morning drink,
The soft pull toward something new.

It's not urgency or pressure this time.
Its gentler, like your soul remembering what it
Means to reach for something simply because
It feels right.
It might be curiosity.
It might be the small spark that says, "I still care."

You don't have to chase it.
You just let it show up.

Feeling alive again doesn't mean the pain is gone.
It means you've learned how to live beside it.
It means your heart can hold both loss and hope
Without breaking from either.

The spark isn't here to erase what hurt you.
It's here to remind you that you're still becoming-
That life still moves through you,
Still wants you to be part of it.

So tonight, if you feel quiet pull toward something simple-
A movie, a breath, a moment of stillness-follow it.
It's not about results.
It's about return.

This is your soul remembering what it means to be alive-
Not just enduring but existing in full again.
testing the light,
learning that it's safe here now.

You've carried enough darkness to know the
light isn't always loud.
Sometimes it's the smallest spark,
guiding you gently back to yourself-
a quiet lamp placed nearby, steady and unassuming,
reminding you that warmth still exists.

You don't have to know what's next.
You just have to stay open to it.

Because beginning again
isn't about starting over.

It's about continuing—
with gentleness,
with strength,
and with the simple truth
that you're still becoming.

With you in the gentle return,
Delilah

Letter Fifty-Eight: You're Still Becoming

Dear Sleepless One,

Theres a shift that happens quietly-
not with applause,
not with a breakthrough,
but with a breath that feels a little lighter than the last.

The world hasn't changed.
But you have.
You start to see yourself again-
not the version shaped by loss or survival,
but the one who's learning to live with both.

You laugh one afternoon and realize it wasn't forced.
You look in the mirror and don't flinch at the reflection.
You catch yourself singing a song without
even thinking about it.
Its subtle, but it's there-
the return of something you thought you'd lost forever.
You're not chasing purpose anymore.
You're living it.
It shows up in how you move through the day-
how you honor your own rhythm instead of
rushing to match anyone else's.

This isn't the loud kind of healing.
It's quiet, steady, deliberate.
It's the way you stop needing proof you're doing enough.
The way you trust that being here, being you,
Is already more than enough.

You used to wait for a miracle.
But maybe the miracle was always you-
The woman who kept showing up,

Who kept breathing,
Who kept rebuilding even when no one was watching.

There comes a time when you stop waiting for a miracle.
Not out of bitterness, not because you've given up-
but because you've learned to live in what remains.

The miracle isn't always what arrives.
Sometimes it's the fact that you're still here,
Breathing without reaching,
Finding peace in a life that stayed when so much else didn't.

You stopped asking when and started whispering now.
And in that small, steady shift,
you found something even quieter than hope-
you found yourself.

With you in the quiet enough,
Delilah

Letter Fifty-Nine: Quiet Return to Yourself

Dear Sleepless One,

There came a point
when peace stopped being a luxury
and became a boundary.

You learned the hard way
that not everyone respects your peace—
some people only understand chaos.
So, you stopped explaining it.
You just started leaving quietly.

You no longer chase understanding.
You no longer stay where your nervous system begs you to go.
You honor what your body knows before your mind can justify it.

Because peace isn't found—
it's protected.
And home isn't a place you escape to.
It's the person you return to you.

There was a time you would've called that selfish.
Now, you know it's sacred.

You've carried enough weight to understand
that energy is currency.
And you can't keep spending yourself
on what keeps you small.

You no longer let guilt be the price of peace.
You no longer confuse kindness with endurance.
You know when to walk away—
not out of anger,
but out of love for yourself.

Your home is quiet now,
not because nothing happens,
but because you've learned to control what you allow in.

Your peace is selective.
Your energy is intentional.
Your door stays open for what's safe
and closes quickly for what's not.

You don't owe anyone access to your stillness.
You've earned it.
You've bled for it.
You've built it from ashes and solitude.

And you're not trading it away again.

So when the world feels loud,
when people pull at pieces of you
that no longer belong to them—
come home.

Sit in your space.
Light your peace.
Remember that you don't need permission
to protect what you've rebuilt.

You are your own sanctuary.
Your own grounding.
Your own safe place to land.

Peace lives here—
not because life stopped being hard,
but because you no longer leave yourself
behind to make others comfortable.

You've learned to return to yourself quietly-
without apology, without explanation,
without guilt.

Because this steady, quiet wholeness—
is what you survived for.

With you in the quiet you built,
Delilah

Letter Sixty: When Feeling Feels Safe

Dear Sleepless One,

You've been cautious with peace.
Careful with calm.
For so long, you associated stillness with the storm that followed.
Every moment of comfort made you tense,
waiting for the next crash.

You didn't mean to stop trusting good things—
you just learned that happiness could vanish without warning.
So you stopped reaching for it.
You stopped expecting it to stay.

But lately, something has shifted.
Peace doesn't scare you as much anymore.
You catch yourself laughing
and don't immediately check what's waiting to go wrong.

You let yourself exhale,
and nothing breaks.

This is new ground—
the space between surviving and living.
The place where your body finally believes
that ease can exist without consequence.

You can smile now
without guilt whispering in the background.
You can rest
without wondering if you've earned it.
You can feel light
without apologizing to the weight you used to carry.

Because peace isn't borrowed anymore.

It's yours.

You've outgrown the need to prove you're okay.
You simply are.
Not because everything is perfect,
but because you've stopped letting pain be the only proof of depth.

You can be wise *and* happy.
You can be healed *and* human.
You can carry love for what's gone
and still make room for what's here.

That's not forgetting.
That's balance.

The truth is—
you deserve softness.
You deserve ease.
You deserve moments that make you laugh
until your stomach aches again.

And you don't have to brace for the moment they end.
You can just live them,
in all their imperfect ways,
without waiting for the fall.

This is peace that stays.
This is the gentle calm before the joy.

And when joy comes,
you'll be ready.
Not because you forced it—
but because you finally know
it's safe to let it in.

With you in the living proof,
Delilah

Letter Sixty-One: When Light Finds You

Dear Sleepless One,

You made it here—
to the part no one talks about enough.
The part after the ache.
After the rebuilding.
After the silence.

The part where peace starts to feel light,
and joy no longer feels like betrayal.

You spent so long surviving
that ease feels almost foreign now.
But it's yours.
You've earned every drop of it.

This is what freedom looks like.
Not perfection.
Not constant happiness.
Just *permission*.

Permission to be whole
without having to prove you're healed.
Permission to laugh
without guilt tugging at your chest.
Permission to dance in your kitchen
with music blaring,
hair messy,
and a drink in your hand—
because you can.

Because you survived everything that
tried to break you.

You don't owe anyone an apology
for feeling amazing again.

You don't need to explain
why you're smiling more,
why you're choosing differently,
why you finally look like peace.

You've cried enough.
You've grieved enough.
You've carried enough.

Now it's time to *live enough.*

To make new memories
without worrying that the old ones will fade.
To look forward
without fearing you're forgetting.
To wake up
and not brace for the day.

You're allowed to enjoy this part—
the becoming that happens after survival.

There's still softness in you,
but it's not weakness anymore.
It's wisdom.
It's balance.
It's grace.

You can love without losing yourself.
You can feel without falling apart.
You can move without hesitation.

You don't rush what's next.
You trust that it will meet you when you're ready.

And in the meantime—
you dance.
You laugh.
You build.
You rest.
You live.

This is what healing was always leading you toward—
not the end of grief,
but the beginning of *you.*

Wild.
Free.
Peaceful.
Unapologetically living.

And when the world sees you now—
when they ask how you survived,
how you kept going,
how you found your way back—
you can simply smile and say:
"Because I did. I chose to."

And that's the truth, isn't it?
You didn't just survive the night.
You learned how to live again at 3 AM,
when the world was still and your heart refused to quit.

This time, you're not afraid of what
tomorrow can bring.
And no one can take that from you.

With you in the rising,
always,
Delilah

ABOUT THE AUTHOR

Delilah Klug writes from the quiet spaces most people never speak about — the hours between night and morning when everything feels heavy, but you're still breathing through it.

After losing her husband, Delilah found herself rebuilding a life she never expected to live, learning how to carry grief in one hand and hope in the other. Writing became the place where she could tell the truth — not the polished version, but the raw, human, midnight version.

Her earlier books, Grief Changed Me: Grace Saved Me and Grief Changed Me: A Widow's Heartbeat, hold the deeper layers of her story — the kind of honesty that only comes from walking through the fire and finding a way to rise again.

3 AM Grief is different.
It was written in the quiet hours, when the world is still but your heart is loud.
These letters don't try to fix anything.
They simply sit beside you — steady, soft, and human.

Delilah writes for anyone who has ever felt alone in their healing, for the ones who carry their thoughts in silence, and for the hearts that keep going even when they're tired. Her words offer comfort without pressure, hope without demands, and companionship without expectation.

When she isn't writing, Delilah is raising her children, honoring her husband's legacy, and building an empire rooted in truth, resilience, and love. Her deepest intention is simple:

That her words become a light in someone else's darkest hour — a reminder that even at 3 AM,
you are not alone.

www.ingramcontent.com/pod-product-compliance
Lightning Source LLC
Chambersburg PA
CBHW060421130626
46555CB00005B/2167